A
BOOK
ABOUT
SMUGGLING
IN
THE
WEST
COUNTRY
1700 — 1850

A Book About SMUGGLING in the West Country, 1700–1850.

by

Antony D. Hippisley Coxe

TABB HOUSE

First published in 1984
Tabb House, 11 Church Street, Padstow, Cornwall

Printed in Great Britain by A. Wheaton and Co. Ltd., Hennock Road,
Marsh Barton, Exeter, Devon.

CONTENTS

List of Illustrations

Tailpieces from wood engravings by T. Bewick.

Frontispiece reproduced by kind permission of John Spedding, cover photograph by Exeter Maritime Museum, and illustrations on pages 2, 14 and 47 by the Cornwall County Local Studies Library. Ballads in Chapter 5 are reproduced from the collection of Tish Stubbs and Sam Richards by their courtesy.

FOREWORD

THIS BOOK really started as an exhibition; but as my researches led me more deeply into the history and techniques of smuggling, as well as the efforts made by the authorities to put a stop to it, the more fascinating facts did I discover. Many of them could not readily be translated into a visual display, which ideally should tell its story without having to resort to lengthy captions. A book, on the other hand, usually does rely on words. So one can compliment the other. This does not mean that the exhibition *requires* a book, any more than this book needs an exhibition. Both stand on their own.

What I hope to achieve here is first to provide the background and describe the techniques of smuggling in the West Country in the eighteenth and nineteenth centuries, which will naturally include the measures taken to try to prevent it; then, against this background, present five famous West Country smugglers. They have been chosen to show the widely different types who were involved in running contraband, and also to represent the various regions of the peninsula, north, south, and west.

My research included visiting a great number of places, interviewing people both in person and by post, spending much time in searching through the files of old newspapers and reading many, many books. I am therefore indebted to a great number of people. Amongst them J. C. Corin, R. Glossop, Miss E. Fryer, John Spedding, Mrs T. Hare, Geoffrey Copinger, Michael Nix, Mrs A. Hamilton and Tish Stubbs.

When it comes to authors, I can only say that all the thirty-seven books in the Bibliography have given me pleasure. At least a third have also been particularly useful and I am most grateful to these authors for teaching me so much. I had hoped that I might give the source of each fact in a footnote, but I discovered that the footnotes were becoming almost as long as the text. This was further complicated by finding what was basically the same story, but with differences, in detail, in several sources. It would, however, be churlish not to acknowledge the importance of *The Nightingale Scandal*, by Stanley Thomas. This meticulously researched little volume, published by the Bideford Gazette in 1959, has become extremely rare. I would also like to draw attention to *Smuggling in Cornwall*, by Cyril Noall, the books of Commander the Hon. Henry Shore afterwards Lord Teignmouth, and *Smuggling*, by David Phillipson. The story of the Customs Service is very fully covered in *Something to Declare*, by Graham Smith.

Finally I would like to thank the staff of the Local Studies Library in Exeter for their unfailing assistance and for making photocopies of many columns of the *Exeter Flying Post* and other newspapers; and my wife who saved me from many solecisms. To all these, and many more, my most grateful thanks.

A.D.H.C.
Ackworthy, Hartland, Devon.

Thought by his descendants to be a portrait of Isaac Gulliver

Chapter 1

THE BACKGROUND

THE WILD and remote coasts of Devon and Cornwall, the hidden caves and coves of Somerset and Dorset, and the rugged individualism of the inhabitants made the West Country famous for smuggling over a period of nearly a thousand years. Smuggling is mentioned in Magna Carta, which refers to wine 'prisage' and the export of wool. In fact, in the early days, preventing wool being smuggled *out* of the country was more important than stopping contraband coming *in*. The men who indulged in this illicit export trade came to be known as 'owlers', though nobody seems to know precisely why; perhaps it was because, like most smugglers, they worked at night. In 1275, duty of half a mark – the equivalent today of 33p. – was imposed on every sack of wool shipped abroad.

Penalties were severe; Florentine merchants, who failed to pay the sum due on 4,000 sacks, were fined £2,200. In 1337 the export of wool was banned altogether. Thirty-seven years later exports were allowed, but again subject to duty. Chaucer, then Comptroller in the port of London, received £71.4s.6d. as his share of the value of wool that had been forfeited because duty had not been paid.

Tin and copper were also smuggled out of Cornwall in pilchard boats – some say as much as 75% of the total production. Later, grain was smuggled out of Barnstaple; and a customs searcher, called Richard Norwood, owned a large barn near Hartland Point in which the grain was collected and stored, before being illegally shipped overseas.

The running of contraband, however, soon became more concerned with imports than exports, though the latter was never completely abandoned, and between 1700 and 1850 it was

The Lizard, from Kinans Cove, c. 1804

sufficiently important to earn West Country smugglers the name of 'free-traders'.

Most people associate smuggling with the south coast of the peninsula, which is, after all, nearer to the Continent. But for this very reason, it has always been more closely watched than the north coast of Cornwall, Devon, and Somerset. As early as the fourteenth century the Severn Sea and Bristol Channel were notorious for their smuggling activities. In 1387 the Mayor of Bristol was instructed to investigate the smugglers entering the estuary, and thirty-four years later Bristol was the first city to have her own customs vessel; it cost £22.6s.7d. Down along the coast the traces still remain today in place names such as Smuggler's Hole, Smuggler's Leap, Samson's Cove, Brandy Cove and Tea Caverns...

In 1597 contraband landed in Mount's Bay and St Ives included: 'Portingalle salt and earthen pottery and Buttes of

Canary wyne called Muskadelle.' By the seventeenth century the emphasis had changed. James I loathed tobacco, which he considered 'an abomination of the Devil'. In an effort to stamp out smoking, he raised the import duty from 2d. to 6s. 6d. a pound, and, although this was reduced to 1s. eighteen years later, smuggling was still worthwhile.

By the beginning of the eighteenth century Bideford was importing more tobacco than any other port in England, with the possible exception of London. It was brought over from our American colonies, Maryland and Virginia, in hogsheads; and these barrels when empty were used as dustbins by the inhabitants. In fact, as Muriel Goaman points out in her book *Old Bideford and District*, this led to Bideford becoming the first town in the kingdom to organise the collection of household refuse.

At the point where the Bristol Channel becomes the Severn Sea lies the island of Lundy, which has been associated with smuggling since the earliest times. A customs collector at Cardiff, quoted by Graham Smith in his history of the Customs and Excise Service, *Something to Declare*, stated quite categorically in the eighteenth century that, 'There never lived yet a man on the island of Lundy who was not connected with smuggling.' In 1700 there were Customs sloops at Weymouth, Dartmouth, Fowey, Penzance, Padstow, Cardiff, and Ilfracombe. Yet it was the Collector of Customs at Ilfracombe at the end of the century who stated that most of the Bristol Channel pilot cutters were running contraband, and that the *Lundy Pilot, Hero*, and *Bristol Galley* did nothing else. Nor was Lundy the only island in the Bristol Channel that served as a smuggling base. Barry Island was first fortified by a smuggler called Knight, who later made Lundy his headquarters; and Flat Holme, where the cave in the east face of the cliff is still called Smuggler's Hole, was the lair of a Guernsey smuggler, the hull of whose ship was painted red, and carried a mermaid as a figurehead. She brought rum, brandy, and tobacco from the Channel Islands, round Land's End and up to the island off the Somerset Coast. A paper in the Public Records Office lists Clovelly as a principal place for landing contraband and describes it as 'notorious for smuggling,' in the nineteenth century.

In fact, there is hardly a cove, creek or island round the whole south and west of England that has not at some time been used by smugglers. In 1724 Daniel Defoe found 'no foreign commerce except it be what we called smuggling and roguing, which, I may say, is the reigning commerce from the mouth of the Thames to the Land's End of Cornwall.' In 1783 a Parliamentary Committee reported that 300 English vessels were *continuously* engaged in smuggling. This did not include foreign smacks, Post Office packets, East Indiamen, vessels engaged in coastal trade, or fishing boats which occasionally indulged in this activity. Although fishing boats might 'run the odd cargo' the East Indiamen, Post Office smacks, and foreign smacks contributed substantially to the goods smuggled into the country. It was estimated that between 1780 and 1783, 2,000,000 lbs of tea and 13,000,000 gallons of brandy had been smuggled.

Smugglers were active all round the coast, but those of Kent and Sussex were a villainous lot compared with those of the West Country. London was their market, and bands such as the Hawkhurst and Ruxley gangs were as brutal a set of ruffians as you would ever find in Newgate. They did, on occasion, venture as far west as Dorset; and it was the Hawkhurst gang who raided the Customs House at Poole to retrieve thirty-seven cwt of tea, valued at £500, which had been seized by revenue officers. That episode led to the appalling murder of Chater, the informer, and Galley, the Riding Officer sent to bring him in as a witness. Both men were beaten almost to death; Galley was then buried alive and Chater thrown down a dry well where large stones were dropped on him until he expired. These dreadful acts led eventually to the hanging of seven of the gang for murder and others for taking part in the raid. No West Country smuggler was as depraved as this, although from time to time they did come into fatal conflict with the Customs Service, as this cutting from the *Exeter Flying Post* for 29th November, 1787, shows.

WHITEHALL, Nov. 16th, 1787.

WHEREAS it has been humbly reprefented to the King, that on Friday Evening, the 2nd Day of November Inftant, a moft inhuman Murder was committed on the bodies of William Jenkins and William Scott, late Officers in his Majefty's Excife, by a Gang of Smugglers, when the faid Officers were in the Execution of their Duty, in attempting to feize fome Run Goods, at a Place called Roncombe's Girt, on the Road between Honiton and Beer, in the County of Devon.

His Majefty, for the better apprehending and bringing to Juftice the Perfons concerned in the faid inhuman Murder, is hereby pleafed to promife his moft gracious Pardon to any one of them (except William Voifey, and any other who may be apprehended prior to the Date of this Advertifement) who fhall difcover his Accomplices therein, fo that they may be apprehended and convicted thereof.

SYDNEY.

And, as a farther Encouragement; the Commiffioners of Excife do hereby promife a reward of TWO HUNDRED POUNDS to any Perfon or Perfons making fuch Difcovery, (except as before excepted) to be paid by their Secretary on conviction of any one or more of the Offenders.

W. JACKSON, pro sec.

These smugglers, you will notice, murdered officers of His Majesty's Excise. Customs and Excise have been closely associated throughout history, although it was not until 1909 that they were officially amalgamated. Sometimes their respective functions seem inextricably mixed; but, as a general rule, customs are concerned with obtaining duty on goods coming into this coutry, and Excise with duty on goods manufactured here. Brandy is liable to Customs duty, whisky to Excise duty. The difficulty arises out of goods such as tobacco, which would be subject to Customs duty when imported, but Excise when manufactured into cigarettes, cigars, snuff, and so on. In this case, it was subject to Customs duty in 1602 and Excise duty in 1978. But you will still have to declare it as you 'go through Customs.'

Tobacco and brandy are the best-known items of contraband; followed, amongst those who remember Rudyard Kipling's verse, by 'laces for a lady' and 'letters for (or perhaps from) a spy.'. . . Actually, in 1815 no less than 1,425 items were subject to duty, including handkerchiefs, Leghorn hats, and playing cards. The tax on playing cards lasted from 1711 until 1960.

If one walked down the High Street of any English town in the eighteenth or early nineteenth century practically every item in the windows of the wine merchant's, tobacconist's, grocer's and draper's shops *could* have been smuggled. In those days smugglers were concerned with everyday goods that were openly available. The important difference between smuggling then and now is that those who run contraband today deal in goods which are not *and never should be* available to the general public, because they do untold harm, particularly narcotics and arms.

The heyday of smuggling was from 1700 to 1850, and during those years the duty on many items varied considerably. When the duty was high it paid to smuggle, when it was reduced on certain goods, it became more profitable to select another line. It is for this reason that one cannot take any one moment of time as typical; to give a broad picture one must generalise. Let us study those shop windows in the High Street in more detail. At the end of the eighteenth century, when the duty on tobacco was 2s. 10d. a pound, it could be got from a smuggler for 1s. 3d., less than half the duty alone, because he could buy it on the Continent for 3d. a pound. In 1784 the country lost £3,000,000 in unpaid duty simply on tobacco. It was said that for every ounce of duty-paid tobacco, one pound was successfully smuggled.

Brandy could be bought in France for 5s. a gallon, and smugglers found a ready market for it at 25s., because when duty had been paid it would cost 32s. William of Orange was responsible for introducing gin to England from Holland, and it became very popular. It cost 2s. a gallon in Holland, but after duty had been paid in England the price was 8s.; smugglers could sell it for 5s. and still make a handsome profit. Port and sherry were cheaper, and although they showed a similar proportion of profit to spirits, they took up just as much space on board a lugger, and smugglers preferred the higher net profit to be obtained from spirits, inspite of the greater capital required. The smuggling of French wine stopped almost overnight in 1786, when Pitt cut the duty by more than half, from £90. 3s. 10d. a tun to £43. 1s.

At one time smugglers tried bringing extra strength brandy into the country and letting it down to the correct alcoholic content over here. The French merchants even supplied caramel free, so that the dark colour could be maintained. This certainly saved space aboard ship, but it led to a shortage of containers, and smugglers went back to the 'half-anker', a tub holding four and a half gallons, and brandy or gin of the ordinary strength.

Few people have any idea of the enormous amount of brandy 'run'. In 1770 it was estimated that 470,000 gallons of 'Cousin Jack'*, as brandy was called amongst free-traders, was smuggled into Cornwall alone. Some years later the Emperor Napoleon stated that 40-50,000,000 francs-worth of brandy and silk were being smuggled out of France into England every year.

Although the salt, pepper, coffee, cocoa, sugar, and spices such as cardamom, turmeric, sesame, mace, and cloves in the grocer's shop could well have been smuggled, by far the largest item of contraband here was tea. Tea-drinking had become immensely popular during the eighteenth century. By 1768 90% of the population, which then numbered 7,000,000, drank tea twice a day; but very few drank tea on which duty had been paid. It was drunk in all strata of society; the working classes usually drank Bohea; the middle classes, Singlo or Hyson; while the upper classes preferred Congo. At this time the duty stood at 4s. 9d. a pound, and the legal price was between 7s. and 10s. a pound. Smugglers could supply for 5s. tea which could be bought on the Continent for 2s. and which cost no more than 6d. in China.

* 'Cousin Jack' may possibly have been rhyming slang for cognac. It became a nickname applied to all Cornishmen, presumably through their smuggling activities, and was taken by Cornish miners to America.

The duty on tea was one of those which fluctuated most widely between 1700 and 1850. The Commutation Act of 1784, for instance, reduced the duty from 119% to 12½% *ad valorem* with one stroke of the pen; yet by 1806 it had risen again to 96%. When duty was low, of course, smuggling virtually ceased; but as the Government had to find the money somehow, other taxes were introduced. Although the Commutation Act lowered the duty on tea, it led to the ridiculous tax on windows. This reduction in duty also largely contributed to the failure of the Scandinavian East India Companies, for they carried a good deal of the tea supplied to English smugglers. And this amounted to 3,000,000 lbs in 1750 and 7,000,000 lbs in 1773. Four years later, when Hyson tea was 14s.–15s. a pound, Parson Woodforde wrote in his diary: 'March 29th. Andrews the smuggler, brought this night, about 11 o'clock, a bagg of Hyson tea, 6 pound weight. He frightened us a little by whistling under the Parlour window just as we were going to bed. I gave him some Geneva and paid him for the tea at 10s. 6d. a pound.'

When smuggling virtually came to an end in the middle of the last century, we were consuming 50,521,384 lbs of tea a year; and the revenue from duty on tea alone amounted to £5,500,000 per annum.

Sometimes the tea was tansferred from a homeward bound east Indian to a smuggling lugger in mid-Channel. William Hickey, in his *Memoirs*, describes such a scene. It took place on the morning of 19th April, 1770.

The 18th we struck soundings in seventy fathoms, and the following morning had the pleasure to see a fine English cutter of one hundred and fifty tons burden within a quarter of a mile of us, from which a man came in a small boat on board the *Plassey*. He was of a Herculean form, with a healthy ruby face. From his dress and appearance I should not have supposed he possessed ten pounds in the world. Captain Waddell conducted him into the round house, where the following short dialogue ensued:

STRANGER: "Well, Captain, how is tea?"

CAPTAIN: "Twenty pounds."

STRANGER: "No, that won't do; eighteen — a great number of China ships this season."

CAPTAIN: "Very-well, you know best."

STRANGER: "How many chests?"

CAPTAIN: "Sixty odd."

STRANGER: "Come, bear a hand then and get them into the cutter."

By this I found our new visitor was a smuggler. The foregoing was all that passed in completing the sale and purchase of so large a quantity of tea. In the same laconic manner he bought the stock of the different officers.

While the tea was hoisting out of the gun room and other places it had been stowed in, Captain Waddell asked the smuggler whether there was any public news, to which he at first answered:

"No, none that I know of"; but immediately after, as if recollecting himself, he added, "Oh yes, I forgot, Wilkes is made King."

"Wilkes made King!" exclaimed everyone present. "What can you mean?"

"Damn me if I understand much of these things," replied the man, "but they told me the mob took him out of prison and made him King — that's all I know."

A thick haze that had prevailed all the morning just then cleared away, and we saw the land (the Lizard) not more than four leagues distant [twelve miles]. The cutter at the same time hailed to inform their chief they saw the *Albert* (custom-house schooner) to the southward.

"Do you, by God," replied he, and taking a spying glass from one of the officers, looked through it in the direction pointed out, directly saying, "Aye, aye, sure enough there she comes and under a cloud of canvas." Turning to Captain Waddell, he continued, "Come, Captain, you must haul off the land another league or so, and then let him fetch us with all my heart, and kiss my a--e."

Captain Waddell appearing to hesitate as to complying, the man hastily said,

"He can seize me at this distance from our coast. If, therefore, you don't stand further off, I must leave you."

Captain Waddell then desired the officer of the watch to brace the yards and keep the ship up a couple of points, which being done, in an hour and a half the smuggler said:

"Now, Captain, let them come and be damned, you may keep your course again."

The schooner was then within two miles, and in another hour came dashing by close to us in a noble style, and hove to upon our weather bow, when a most capital exchange of naval blackguardism took place between the smuggler's crew and the schooner, continuing a full hour; but, as the *Plassey* was then beyond the stated limits, they could not molest the cutter, and remained only to have the mortification of seeing a large quantity of goods transferred from the ship to her. At length they sheered off, when the smuggler observed:

"The fellow that commands her is one of the damnedest scoundrels that lives, and the only rascal amongst them that I cannot deal with, though I have bid roundly too." (I do not remember the name of this extraordinary revenue officer, or I would mention it, as, I am afraid, a rare instance of integrity in his line.)

Captain Waddell asked the smuggler whether he had recently sustained any loss by the Government vessels, to which he answered:

"No, nothing material this long time. I had a seizure of between five and six hundred pounds ten days ago, but nothing of importance for a twelvemonth"; by which it was evident he considered five or six hundred pounds no object.

The tea being all removed to the cutter, pen, ink, and paper was produced; the smuggler sitting down at a table in the round house, calculated the amount due for his purchase; which Captain Waddell admitting correct, he took from his pocket-book a cheque, which filled up for twelve hundred and twenty-four pounds he signed and delivered it to the captain. I observed it was drawn upon Walpole and Company, Bankers in Lombard Street, and was astonished to see Captain Waddell with the utmost composure deposit it in his escritoire. The smuggler then being asked whether he chose a glass of wine or would stay dinner, he answered he could not afford to lose a minute; so must be off; but would take a *drap* of brandy. The liquor being brought, he chucked off a bumper, the servant directly filling a second. "That's right, my good fellow," said he, "always wet both eyes." He swallowed the second and returned to his cutter. The moment he departed, I asked Captain Waddell whether he felt secure in a draft for so large a sum by such a man as that; to which he answered, "Perfectly, and wish it was for ten times as much; it would be duly paid. These people always deal with the strictest honour. If they did not, their business would cease." For what he purchased from the officers he paid in guineas, to the amount of upwards of eight hundred. ...

Furthermore, it was not always necessary for deals with East Indiamen to be completed at sea. In 1763 three East Indiamen, lying in Falmouth harbour sold £20,000-worth of China tea, arrack, handkerchiefs, etc., direct to the inhabitants *without a single item passing through the Customs*.

With smuggling taking place on such a vast scale, one can appreciate the report from Newquay that in 1775 it was no uncommon thing for 100 horses, on Sundays as well as weekdays, to be waiting for contraband; and there is no doubt that this could be said of many other places both in and outside the West Country. After all, one night in 1748 the smugglers from Hastings and Deal loaded 11½ tons of contraband on 350 horses.

West Country smugglers were known as free-traders, because this is precisely what they were. Smuggling was not simply a question of bringing brandy, tobacco and so on back from France; it meant taking goods over the Channel from England, too. Cotton stockings, costing 1s. a pair over here could be sold for 5 francs; needles bought for 1d a dozen would fetch a franc, while threepenny files made 1 franc and 30 centimes. Woollen goods also showed a good profit; and an anvil priced at £3 over here brought in the equivalent of £7 in France. With the proceeds from such sales the smugglers bought their contraband—or at least some of it. Perhaps the most reprehensible activity was smuggling gold out of England. There had been a financial crisis in France in 1784, which placed gold at a premium. Then Napoleon needed gold to pay his armies. At one time this country was losing £1,000,000 worth of gold a year. Between 10,000 and 12,000 guineas were leaving England each week, in galleys often rowed across the Channel from Sussex and Kent. These 'guinea galleys' were built in Calais and powered by as many as 36 oarsmen. They were so fast that for a revenue cutter to give chase was said to be like 'sending a cow to catch a hare.'

With smuggling reaching such formidable proportions one wonders what the Revenue Service and Customs officers were doing. Although a remarkable amount of contraband seems to have slipped through, they did enjoy some success. Here are the figures for a selection of goods seized in 1822–24:

Tobacco	902,684½	lbs
Snuff	3,000	lbs
Brandy	130,000	gallons
Rum	253	gallons
Gin	227,900	gallons
Tea	19,000	lbs
Silk	42,000	yds.
Handkerchiefs	2,400	
Playing cards	3,600	packs
Leghorn hats	23	

Chapter 2

ORGANISATION & OPERATION

FREE-TRADING, as described in the last chapter, would help the individual fisherman with a small boat to raise capital with which to buy contraband in France. But it would take many thousand pairs of cotton stockings or gross of needles to finance a big expedition. The more successful smuggling became, the bigger it grew, and the bigger it grew, the more organisation was required on both sides of the Channel. Although running contraband in the West of England was not in the hands of recognised bands as it was in Kent and Sussex, there was a definite pattern in operational procedure, and certain families became identified with particular aspects of the enterprise.

First there was the 'venturer'. This was the man who put up the capital, the investor. He was usually a man of substance and position, such as a landowner, who remained anonymous, particularly if he was also a local magistrate. He would commission the captain of a smuggling vessel to cross the Channel and bring back whatever was required. Although alternative landing places may have been discussed before the vessel sailed, the exact position of Customs Offices on land, or revenue cutters offshore, at the time of arrival could not be foreseen, so the landing was the responsibility of the 'spotsman', who signalled the vessel in when the coast was clear. 'The coast is clear' is in itself a smuggling phrase, while 'a flash in the pan' was the signal made by a special pistol to inform the captain that it was safe to land. The word 'bootlegger' originally referred to smugglers who brought tobacco ashore inside their sea boots, while another word which was originally used by revenue men is 'rummage', which meant to search for contraband. Other signals were made at night by spout lanterns, which showed a pinpoint of light in one direction only, flares, and sometimes even

Mevagissey c. 1813

by braziers. If the landing was made by day, smoke was often used, or the signal might be made by a man riding, say, a grey horse in a certain direction. These signals not only meant that it was safe to land, but that transport was also ready to carry the goods to the hiding place.

If the cargo consisted of brandy, this would have been shipped in the small tubs known as half-ankers. They were roped together in pairs so that they could be carried up the cliff, lying across the chest and shoulders of the 'tub-carriers'. As each half-anker weighed over 50 lbs, a tub-carrier was not able to defend himself very well if attacked. He was therefore protected by 'batmen', who were usually armed with staves and cudgels, but occasionally carried fire-arms. At the top of the cliff horses and carts or pack ponies would be waiting to carry the contraband away inland to the hide. These horses, ponies, and sometimes donkeys and mules too, were occasionally shaved and covered with lard or soap. Another trick employed by carters was to train these draught-horses to obey the opposite command. 'Whoa!' and 'Stop!' meant 'Go like the wind!' Tub-carriers and batmen were paid as little as 1s. or as much as 12s. for a night's work, with tea or brandy, maybe, thrown in, according to the success of the run.

Sometimes neighbouring villages specialised in one aspect of the operation. For instance, down on the south coast of Devon, 'Sidbury financed, Branscombe landed, Sidmouth found waggons and Salcombe the carriers.' The batmen, however, were specialists, and here, as elsewhere, came from Yeovil, which lies a good twenty miles from the coast and over thirty from the scene of these operations. They always blackened their faces and armed themselves with swingle-bats.

The only change in the whole procedure during the period from 1700 to 1850 was in financing the operation, and this occurred in the last decade. Instead of the venturer putting up the money, it became increasingly popular for a group of people to decide on how many tubs should be run, and then take out as many 'shares' as they wished, paying £2 for each tub. Of this, £1 went to pay for the brandy and the other was banked until the brandy was landed. It then went to meet transportation, landing, protection costs and so on. If the cargo was seized by the Customs before landing the investor only lost half his money. The founder of the co-operative movement is usually attributed to the Rochdale Equitable Pioneers in 1844, but it is possible that the Cornish smugglers preceded them.

In 1830 the crew of a smuggling lugger might get between £10 and £25 a trip, if the cargo was large. The captain, of course, got more, and considerably more if he also happened to be the venturer. One pound sterling, in those days, was worth a guinea in France; and a tub of brandy cost 18s., say 4s. a gallon. Added to this the supplier gave one extra barrel in every twenty, known as 'scorage', which was the perquisite of the captain – a 'smuggler's score' rather than a 'baker's dozen'.

The duty on brandy was then 32s. a gallon. Even if one allowed
4s.6d. for the brandy, another 4s.6d. for transport, etc., one could
still make over 100% profit if one sold it at half the duty-paid
price.

The vessels used by smugglers were usually luggers, built at
Mevagissey, Cawsand, and Polperro, because these were shallow-
draft boats which could work close inshore and up tidal estuaries
and creeks. The Customs Service, on the other hand, used
deep-keeled revenue cutters with long bowsprits for speed. But a
smuggling lugger was by no means slow; a Mevagissey boat, with
1,000 square feet of canvas, could cross the Channel in eight
hours given a fair wind. These boats usually carried a dipping lug
mainsail and a standing lug mizzen. They differed slightly from the
smuggling luggers found east of the Isle of Wight. In a Folkstone
lugger, for instance, you would have found the mizzen topsail
higher than the mainsail. The French and Belgian luggers, which
were also used for smuggling, were very different. They often
carried three masts. The distance from the bows to the foremast
would be ⅛th to ¹⁄₁₀th the total length of the vessel; the mainmast
was much taller than the foremast and carried a standing lug with
the tack close to the mast, and a leg-o' mutton mizzen. The most
popular of these were known as *chasse-marées*.

Galleys were also built at Mevagissey, with a beam one sixth of
the length. They were usually rowed, but a mast could be stepped
dead amid-ships to carry an almost rectangular sail, with one third
of the yard forward of the mast. The Guinea Boats, which took
gold over to France from the South-east coast were also known as
'The Death'.

Most of the West Country smuggling luggers were of 15 to 20
tons, though some were very much bigger. *Sweepstake* was a ship
of 250 tons, armed with 26 guns – nine and twelve-pounders –
and carrying a crew of 50. One must however be careful not to
equate such figures with today's tonnage. Before 1835, according
to John B. Cornish, tonnage was calculated by subtracting three
fifths of the maximum beam from the length of the keel,

multiplying this by the beam and this result by half the beam; divided the result by 94, and the answer is the size of the ship in tons!

How much contraband the average smuggling lugger could carry depended on whether or not the cargo was hidden. False bilges, double bulkheads, secret cuddies, and hollow spars were common. In August, 1841, towards the end of the smuggling era, tobacco was still being hidden in sails and bunks, as this cutting shows:

Exeter Flying Post. September 2nd.

PLYMOUTH – On the 21st ult. the sloop *Five Brothers*, of this port, Wm. Masters, master, through the vigilance of Capt. Potbury and the crew of the *Busy* cutter, was seized in Pomphlet Lake, near the Laira Bridge, Catwater, and there was found concealed in the bed-places and under the sails, 126 bales containing 3,131 lbs of manufactured tobacco, and 6 bales of tobacco stems, weighing 178 lbs. At the time she was boarded by the officers of the *Busy*, the *Five Brothers* was lying a-ground, limestone having been just thrown into her, but there was no one on board, the crew, it is supposed, seeing the officers approaching, having left her. On the 24th, however, Masters, and a man named Hookings, belonging to her were apprehended and, on Friday last, brought before T. Gardner and J. Collier, Esqrs., County Magistrates, at Plymouth. – Mr Eastlake attended on the part of the Crown; and the information against the defendants was exhibited by W. Vanderkiste, Esq., Collector of Customs at Plymouth. – Mr Potbury stated to the Court, that the duty on the tobacco found in the vessel amounted to £1,510.19s. It appeared that she was last from Guernsey, where the tobacco was taken on board. Both defendants pleaded guilty; and Masters said, the mate and himself were the only persons on board the vessel, and they went to Guernsey by accident. He knew the parties to whom he should have delivered the tobacco, and whose property it was, but refused to tell their names; or to say more than that they did not live very far from that place. The bench told him there were circumstances of great aggravation in his case, he being the master of the vessel; he was, therefore, committed to the Devon County Goal for nine calendar months, or until the sum of £100 be paid. Hookings was committed to the same prison for six calendar months. Masters is a married man, with a family; Hookings is young and unmarried.

Sometimes much more elaborate hides were arranged, as can be seen from this report dated 23rd August, 1816:

FRENCH SMUGGLERS IN LOOE

On Thursday last a small French vessel was observed to be nearly on shore, not far from Looe harbour; happily by the exertions of persons belonging to the port, she was got in safely... The vessel is chiefly laden with fruit, and having entered it at the Custom-house at Looe, a great part of the cargo was speedily disposed of. The custom-house officers took particular notice of twelve elegantly formed toys, in the shape of horses, the bodies of which were about four inches in diameter; and on handling them, they were led to suppose that they were more valuable than they appeared to be. Accordingly, one of them was disembowelled, which led to a similar examination of the rest. The result was, the finding of 51 pair of silk stockings and 9 silk shawls which had been carefully secreted in the bodies of these elegant play-things. The King's broad arrow has been placed on the vessel and cargo, in consequence of this unlucky discovery.

However, it was not always necessary to hide contraband on board. Half-ankers were strung together like pearls, weighted with stones, and slung over the ship's bulwarks ready to be dropped to the sea-bed, when a revenue cutter was sighted. This was known as 'sowing the crop'. The spot was either marked or plotted on the chart, so that, once the danger was over, smugglers with 'creepers', which were grapnels, specially designed for a sandy, muddy, or rocky bottom could retrieve the casks.

*   *   *   *

Although Flushing, Dunkirk, and the ports of the Low Countries supplied smugglers on the South-east coast, particularly with gin, Guernsey was the port first favoured by West Country smugglers during the eighteenth century. An ancient charter made it exempt from Customs and Excise. At one time there are said to have been 2,000 coopers on the island making half-ankers for the smugglers. Victor Hugo's house, Hauteville, was said to be furnished entirely by smugglers. The British Government had for many years tried to stamp out smuggling, but the islanders fought every inch of the way to protect their ancient rights. Some of the reasons they put forward for allowing things to continue in the same way many seem rather far fetched today. Guernseymen maintained that the health of the Cornish miners would suffer if they did not have access to smuggled spirits; their work underground made it essential for them to have a tot or two, and they could in no way afford duty-paid prices. They were also convinced that the termination of Guernsey's privileges would not only bring economic ruin to the island, but hand the trade on a plate to our enemy, France.

In 1808 an Act of Parliament brought the Channel Islands under the Customs and Excise laws of the mainland, and much of the trade did indeed go to France. But for some time before that things had been made increasingly difficult for the smugglers. In 1769 a Customs House had been established at St Peter's Port in order to see that no spirit was exported from the island in barrels of less than sixty gallons. This, it was hoped, would prevent brandy from being carried up the cliffs of Dorset, Devon, and Cornwall. No spirit was allowed to be transported in vessels of less than fifty tons, which ruled out most of the smuggling luggers. Although such ridiculous laws could be and were evaded, some smugglers began looking elsewhere, fearing stricter measures might be enforced.

From the fourth century, when British Celts settled in what was then known as Armorica (thereby bequeathing it the name of Brittany), right down to the onion sellers of the twentieth century, the little port of Roscoff has forged surprising links with Great Britain. Mary, Queen of Scots, engaged to the Dauphin at the age of six, landed there. The house where she is reputed to have stayed, and Mary Stuart's Tower, can still be seen. Charles

Edward, the Young Pretender, also landed there, arriving after he had fled from Scotland on 10th October, 1746. But the strangest visitors from these shores must have been those concerned with smuggling. It has been said that Louis XV made Roscoff a free port in 1769; but although the inhabitants seem to be constantly petitioning the authorities in attempts to be relieved of various tolls and taxes, I do not think that it was technically a free port. Professor Jean-Yves Tanguy in his history of the place, *Le Port et Havre de Roscoff*, describes how, after the Anglo-French Treaty of 1786, 'many foreign merchants preferred to emigrate (from Roscoff) to free ports, and the French Revolution did nothing to put the local economy back on its feet. The brief hour of Roscoff's maritime splendour was over.'

That is the French view. For the West Country smuggler Roscoff remained for many years his favourite *entrepôt* port. It is said that here and at Dunkirk, they were given free accommodation. The British Customs Service certainly placed informers in the Brittany town. A report which one of them sent back gives some idea of the volume of trade, even as late as 1832. The vessels arriving between 13th and 31st March and departing between 15th and 27th March in that year were as follows:

Vessel	Tonnage	Cargo	Bound for
Goldfinch of Plymouth	14 tons	90 tubs	Plymouth
Four Brothers of Plymouth	12 tons	20 tubs	Plymouth
Goldfinch of Dartmouth	17 tons	120 tubs	Dartmouth
Supply of Dartmouth	9 tons	60 tubs	Dartmouth
Rose of The Lizard	13 tons	80 tubs	The Lizard
Dove of Cowes	18 tons	125 tubs	Cowes
Eagle of Fowey	35 tons	150 tubs	Fowey
Love of Coverack	26 tons	125 tubs	Coverack
William of Falmouth	13 tons	80 tubs	Falmouth

The report goes on to state that the *Goldfinch* of Plymouth, *Eagle*, and *Dove* sailed on 27th March and were back in Roscoff for another cargo on 31st March, and *Eagle* and *Dove* had the Dunstan Brothers on board. They were amongst the most famous West Country smugglers.

In order to mislead the Customs, false name plates and sometimes false colours were used; but although the names of the vessels may not be genuine, nor their destination, the tonnage as then calculated and cargo is probably accurate, so 3,400 gallons of brandy left Roscoff to be smuggled into England probably between the Isle of Wight and the Lizard, in twelve days.

The English, Scottish, and Irish merchants who supplied these smugglers had been established in Roscoff for many years. Amongst them one finds the names Bagot, Mallaby, de L'Isle, Wege, McCullock, Diot, Biggs, Keith, Gibbs, and Copinger. This last name will figure later in this book. John Copinger's firm had been in Roscoff since 1768 and possibly before. And the staggering amounts of contraband which are reported to have been smuggled into England are confirmed by the merchant's own figures. During the period from 1st October, 1768 to 15th August, 1778, John Copinger's company alone had supplied 3,783,909 lbs of tea and 19,400 *barriques* of brandy. A *barrique* is no half-anker: it is, according to my dictionary, the equivalent of a hogshead, and is the barrel in which the brandy was delivered to the merchant before he transferred it into the more easily transported tubs. Copinger was therefore selling very nearly 2,000 gallons of brandy a week. If we remember that 50 years later 3,200 gallons were still being shipped out of Roscoff in 12 days, Copinger's trade, although surprising, is not at all impossible. Because of their huge turnover Copinger's company appear to have been allowed to trade throughout the American War of Independence, when other English merchants were suspended.

Copinger certainly seems to have been the biggest supplier of contraband in 1785, judging by the taxes he was asked to pay. His assessment was £250, compared with £48 for McCulloch, £36 for Sieurs Biggs, Keith, and Gibbs, £24 for Diot, and £24 for Sieur Katter. Mallaby, Wege, Bagot, and de L'Isle do not appear to have been operating at that time; while Barnett and Stile, two other Englishmen then living in Roscoff, were not merchants but innkeepers, who ran taverns for the smugglers on the waterfront.

The number of expatriates in Roscoff in 1775 can be judged by the action of the Curé, who tried to force the Protestant foreigners to observe the fast days and Lenten vows of the Catholic Church. The importance of smuggling to the economy of the port can equally be seen from the reaction of the Bishop of St Pol de Leon, to whom the matter was referred. In no way, he said, should the over-zealous actions of the parish priest be allowed to prejudice the trade in tea, the value of which amounted to 4,000,000 francs, not to mention brandy, a national product. The foreign Protestant merchants were, therefore, to be given dispensation.

One wonders if the Curé's zeal had been inflamed by Captain Harry Carter, a very famous smuggler and also a staunch Methodist, whose story is told later. He held evangelical services on the quay at Roscoff every Sunday morning for the resident English and visiting smugglers, a sight which may well have kept a number of good Catholics away from Mass.

At one time tobacco, bought in Jersey, was sold in Roscoff rather than England, presumably because during a tobacco shortage, the price was better. Although brandy and tea were the mainstays of the Roscoff trade, the merchants also supplied gin, which was the only foreign spirit they were allowed to hold in bond, and salt, which cost 1½d a lb in France and could be sold in England for 5d. The vast warehouses that lined the wharfs could be entered by water, so that boats could be loaded unseen.

Roscoff was not the only Continental port used by smugglers. Cherbourg was also fairly popular, while those living in Kent and Sussex found other English merchant houses ready to supply their needs, in Dunkirk, Ostend, and Nieuwpoort. Some of these merchants ran their own smuggling vessels; and I believe that Copinger was one of them.

Most people associate smuggling with the coast and imagine caves along the shore filled with contraband. This may be true of the remote parts of the Peninsula, but where Customs officers patrolled the cliffs it was safer to get the contraband inland and distributed as quickly as possible. If you study the map, you will often find a 'Smuggler's Lane' many miles from the sea. One, for instance, runs east from the A350, below Hod Hill, north of Blandford Forum in Dorset. This must be twenty miles from the coast.

Along the smugglers' routes, places where they would be well received were marked by a bottle set in the eaves. You will find one at Batt's Close, Offwell, which lies between Axminster and Honiton. And J. R. W. Coxhead, in *Smuggling Days in Devon* reports another at School House, Wilmington. Batt's Close, it is said, was used by the smugglers of Beer, a very famous centre for running contraband and the home of Jack Rattenbury, the Rob Roy of the West. Sampford Peverell was also on their route; and, like the phantom Drummer of Herstmonceux, smuggling has been given as the explanation of one of Devon's most famous ghosts.

In 1810 ghostly manifestations in this village led to all sorts of enquiries. The Governor of the County Gaol investigated the affair; a £250 reward was offered for an explanation; and the poltergeist-like activities made headlines in the Press. The Reverend Philip Rossiter of Sampford Peverell talked with those who had experienced the rappings and rattlings, the object flying through the air, and the woman's screams. He came to the conclusion that the disturbances were deliberately caused by smugglers. He told the author of *Haunted Houses*, Charles Harper:

When I was in Beer in 1876... I used to visit a very old smuggler – a delightful old man – and he told me many tales of the days of smuggling; how they used to land the spirits on very dark nights, and if pursued by Revenue Officers, take them inland on pack-horses. I asked how far they took their load, and he –not knowing in the least where I came from – said, "Sometimes we took them as far as Sampford Peverell, and hid them in an old tree in the churchyard."

There is an old elm tree here which is of great size, and perfectly hollow, with no entrance except from the top of the trunk.

If they took some of their spirits to the Old Ghost House (which was known to have double walls with a passage in between) they would wish to frighten the people to account for the noise they made in storing them. It appears that at that time there was a rector here whose brother was Rector at Seaton, adjoining Beer; and perhaps they helped the smugglers, as it is a well-known fact that many gentry and parsons in those days did so.

That indeed is true; the vicars of East Budleigh were intimately connected with smuggling for over a hundred years, and in the thickness of the rectory walls there were two secret passages eighteen inches wide.

Certainly there have been hides in graveyard tombs, in church towers, and even pulpits. The octagonal tower at Worle, on the outskirts of Weston-super-Mare, was used for storing contraband; while Uphill church tower, to the south-west of the town, was used for signalling to smugglers that the coast was clear. Ghost stories have been circulated to keep people, particularly inquisitive children, away from hides in several parts of the West Country. One must remember that countyfolk were much more superstitious then than they are now, and children were really frightened by stories of ogres and rhymes such as 'Fee! Fie! Fo! Fum!' In fact, it is my belief that the legend of Cannibals living in a cave at Clovelly, which may well have been a folk memory dating back to the Iron Age Celts, was deliberately resuscitated in order to keep children away from a cave in which there were certainly casks, but not of pickled human flesh, as the story suggests, but of brandy.

The most ingenious place that has come to my notice is that built by Farmer Bray at Woodhead Farm, Branscombe. J. R. W. Coxhead describes it as a 'deep pit beside the cow-shed, across which fair-sized tree-trunks had been laid, and upon this solid foundation Farmer Bray always kept a large rick of hay. The cleverly concealed entrance to the passage leading into the pit passed underneath the cow-shed, and in spite of all the efforts made by the authorities to discover the whereabouts of the hiding place it was never found.'

So much for the places in which the contraband was hidden. It then had to be distributed to the customers. Jack Rattenbury's partner, as we shall see, carried it under the turf and logs he sold around the county. Farmers often carried spirits in pigs' bladders, so that if they happened to be chased by a Customs officer they could pierce the container before they were caught. The women of Cawsand used bladders, too, which they hid under their skirts; while the maids of Devoran, according to Cyril Noall, carried cloam pitchers of water, but with a double bottom which concealed the brandy.

Chapter 3

THE LAW

IF anyone wanted an example of Mr Bumble's dictum, 'The law is a ass,' he could do no better than peruse the Customs regulations of the eighteenth and nineteenth centuries. Above all they show how frantic the authorities were in their vain efforts to stamp out any form of smuggling. I have already described how spirits could only be shipped legally in both barrels and boats of over a certain size in order to prevent the tubs from being carried up cliff paths and luggers slipping up shallow creeks. It would appear from the following advertisement that seized cargoes were put up for auction only in large casks as well.

PORT of PLYMOUTH

By Order of the Honourable Commiffioners of his Majefty's Cuftoms.

On Saturday the 24th of November, 1787, by Ten o'Clock in the Forenoon, will be expofed to Public Sale at the Cuftom Houfe in this Port, for Exportation to Foreign Parts, or for Confumption on board any Ships or Veffels going upon Foreign Voyages, purfuant to the Act of the 26th of his prefent Majefty, Chap. 73d, Sect. 66, and Security to be given for the due Compliance with the Regulations required by the faid Act, the Spirits under-mentioned, viz.

BRANDY					13,945	
RUM					1,237	Gallons
GENEVA					6,074	
CORDIALS					3	

The above Spirits are contained in large Cafks of 70 to 120 Gallons each, and will be fat up in feveral Lots, and fold to the higheft Bidder, subject to the above-mentioned Conditions. Attendance will be given at the Cuftom-houfe aforefaid, for viewing and tafting the fame, Three Days before the Day of Sale.

Cuftom-houfe, dated 6th Nov. 1787.

Capstone Hill Parade, Ilfracombe

The same restriction on the size of containers were applied to tobacco, which, the law stipulated, had to be imported in packages of 450 lbs or more. The hope that dutiable goods would only be unloaded at recognised quays, under the eyes of the Customs, was not fulfilled; spirits, tea, tobacco, silk, lace, and many other items continued to be surreptitiously landed at dead of night in half-ankers and handy packages.

So other laws were passed. Only warships and revenue cutters were permitted to carry long bowsprits. Revenue cutters sometimes carried bowsprits which were almost as long as their hulls, enabling them to hoist more sail and thus produce greater speed. The laws covering bowsprits and flying jibs became extremely complicated, and their significance is difficult to appreciate, particularly when technical terms are obscured in legal phraseology. What actually happened, however, provides an excellent example of the short-sightedness of the law on the one hand and the ingenuity of the smugglers on the other. One of the easiest ways of increasing the area of canvas on a sailing vessel is by extending the bowsprit with a jib-boom. A flying-jib could then be set from the end of this extension to a point well up the mast. When the length of the bowsprit was reduced by law and flying-jibs banned altogether, the smugglers simply turned the sail upside-down, and set it from just above the end of the shortened bowsprit to a point further up the mast. The sail then became a jib-topsail, which was perfectly legal.

At one time, when a smuggling lugger was caught it was put up to auction together with its contraband cargo. The proceeds were then divided fifty-fifty between the Crown and the captain and crew of the vessel that seized her. This was stopped to prevent smugglers from buying back their luggers and continuing their calling. A law was passed by which every boat seized for smuggling had to be sawn in three. This continued for many years, and is probably the origin of Pegotty's house, described by Dickens. A newspaper advertisement for 3rd April, 1832, announced the sale at St Ives of a quantity of glass and a broken hull of a vessel called *Elizabeth*, whose captain had been caught and tried for smuggling three months previously.

One of the strangest laws introduced to stop smuggling was the Hovering Act, which first appeared on the Statute Book in 1718. This made any vessel liable to seizure if it was found outside the area in which it was licensed to operate. The law was amended by Pitt in 1784 to apply to any vessel of less than sixty tons, carrying brandy, tea, wine, coffee, or French silk, hovering within three miles of the coast.

The fact that galleys were used for smuggling meant extending the net to catch rowing boats. So in 1721 any boat with more than four oars, found on the coast, was liable to be cut into three.

It was forbidden to signal to ships off shore with flares or fires or lanterns; the penalty was a month's hard labour. A receiver of smuggled goods could be imprisoned for three months, and the smuggler transported for seven years.

Smuggling not only continued but increased; so the penalties became more severe. The death penalty was introduced. Anyone hiding a smuggler was considered a felon and an outlaw, for which he could be sentenced to death. In 1736 you could be hanged for wounding, or even hindering, a Customs officer; and later this was extended to include shooting at a Naval officer or Revenue patrol.

And smuggling continued.

In desperation other laws were passed. In 1746 a *county* was liable to a fine of £200, if contraband was seized within its borders without the apprehension of the smugglers. If, however, the smugglers were caught during the following six months, then the fine was remitted. Counties were also fined £100 for every Revenue officer killed and £40 for each one bruised within their boundaries. An even heavier fine of £500 could be incurred by the captain of a vessel flying false colours, such as the Admiralty or Customs pennant. On the other hand £500 was also the amount a Customs officer could be fined if he accepted a bribe.

Smugglers who turned informer were pardoned; and, of course, rewards were offered, as this advertisement from the *Exeter Flying Post* shows:

WHITEHALL, October 5, 1791

Whereas it has been reprefented to the Commiffioners of his Majefty's Cuftoms, that on Tuefday the 16th of Auguft laft, the DOLPHIN Revenue Cutter, Rich. John, Commander, ftationed at the Port of St. Ives, fell in with a large armed Smuggling Lugger near Padftow, in the County of Cornwall, when the Smugglers Felonioufly fired a Shot at the Dolphin, brought her to, and immediately ordered Mr. Ofmond, the Mate of the Cutter, on board, who found her navigated with about fifty Men, all armed ready for Action, having eight Six-pounders mounted, with as many more in the Hold, and pierced for eighteen Guns:

His Majefty, for the better difcovering and bringing to Juftice the Perfons concerned in this Felony and Outrage, is hereby pleafed to promife his moft gracious Pardon to any one or more of the faid Offenders who fhall difcover his or their Accomplice or Accomplices there, (except the Mafter or Commander of the faid Lugger, or the Perfon who actually fired) fo that one or more of them may be apprehended and convicted of the faid Offence.

HENRY DUNDAS.

Cuftom-Houfe, London, Oct. 5, 1791.

AND as a further Encouragement the Commiffioners of his Majefty's Cuftoms do hereby promife a Reward of ONE HUNDRED POUNDS to any Perfon or Perfons (except as before excepted) who fhall difcover and apprehend, or caufe to be difcovered and apprehended any one or more of the faid Offenders, to be paid by the Receiver-General of his Majefty's Cuftoms, upon Conviction. By Order of the Commiffioners.

JAMES HUME, Secretary.

When a smuggler was caught and sentenced to transportation, it often happened that the prisoner managed to escape in France and work his way back to England. In 1738 we find a reward of £50 being offered for the apprehension of six smugglers who had been sentenced to transportation just three months previously. As time went by and smuggling continued to flourish the rewards became larger. By 1814 £200 was being offered, and this had increased to £300 by 1828. The highest sums offered as a reward that I have come across was £500.

In 1778 a gaoled smuggler could be released if he found two volunteers for the Navy or Army; while during the American War of Independence he would be set free if he himself joined the Fleet. Those who chose to serve in the Royal Navy rather than a term in prison had their official number preceded by the letters CP which meant they had been handed over by the Civil Powers.

There was also the dreadful custom of offering Revenue officers 'head money' of £20 for every smuggler caught. The smugglers's hatred of the Customs Service was further exacerbated by the fact that they worked in with the Press Gangs. They were empowered to pay 12d. as imprest money, 6d. a day for keep, until enough men had been gathered in, and 8d. a day for each man on the march to the naval depot. Under the heading CADGWITH SMUGGLERS PRESS-GANGED, a newspaper cutting for 26th July, 1816, described how 'the revenue cutter, *Hinde*, sent to Falmouth on Tuesday last a boat belonging to Cadgwith, having

on board 50 ankers of spirit. Four men who were on board the
smuggler have been taken to Plymouth for the purpose of being
put on board the fleet about to sail under Lord Exmouth, against
the Algerines.'

Naturally the organization of the Customs Service changed
over the years between 1700 and 1850. The collection of revenue
in the form of duty had originally been leased out to private
individuals. It was Charles II who set up the first Board of
Customs and planned the service. Gradually an organisational
pattern was evolved. The country was divided into areas and each
area was administered by a Collector. His staff and their duties can
be seen on the diagram on the following page.

The pay changed, too, over the period; but those on land seem
to have enjoyed a higher rate than those at sea. For instance when
those patroling the cliffs were getting £35 p.a. a seaman received
no more than £14.10s. because, it must be presumed, his keep and
prize money would make up the difference. Riding Officers were
sometimes still holding their jobs at the age of eighty, when they
could hardly have been very active in pursuit; while the dragoons,
it is said, could, as often or not, be dissuaded from giving chase by
dropping a keg of spirit in their path.

It was not really until 1822 that the organisation became
clear-cut, when the Coast Guard was set up. Even so, the revenue
cutters and cruisers remained under the Admiralty, who also had
the responsibility of appointing all the officers and men. What
virtually happened was that the three branches, the offshore
revenue cutters, the inshore water guard, and the on-shore riding
officers from a purely operational point of view all came under the
Customs Commissioners. Yet one can still see the influence of the
Admiralty in the new organization. The Riding Officers force was
cut by half; the in-shore craft having been returned to the Customs
was greatly reduced; whereas the revenue cutters which stayed
under Admiralty control became more important. The first
Comptroller-General of the Coast Guard was a Captain in the
Royal Navy.

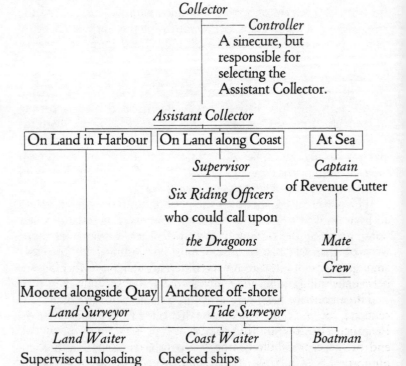

The revenue cutters have always enjoyed pride of place in the fight to prevent smuggling. Their bases in the West Country, and their relative importance, can be seen from the following list of vessels and their compliment in 1784.

Base	Name	Crew
Plymouth.	Ranger.	21
Plymouth.	Wasp.	20
Exeter.	Alarm.	21
Dartmouth.	Spider.	28
Falmouth.	Hawk.	18
Falmouth.	Lark.	20
Penryn.	Lurcher.	30
Scillies.	Tamar.	25
St Ives.	Brilliant.	30
St Ives.	Dolphin.	26

I believe the largest cutter in the Revenue Service was *Greyhound*, a ship of 200 tons with 16 guns and a crew of 43; and the smallest was *Nimble*, which carried a crew of 15. Some Revenue cutters were bought by smugglers and used for running contraband, amongst them were *Rob Roy, Secret,* and *Eliza*; on the other hand I believe the smuggler *Susanna* later served in the Revenue Service.

The number of bases appear to have declined in the eighteenth century, for in 1700 ships were kept at Weymouth, Fowey, Penzance, Padstow, and Ilfracombe, as well as Dartmouth. By the end of the century Ilfracombe seems to have come a forgotten outpost. The Collector there complained that inspite of vast amount of contraband being run in the Bristol Channel there were no more than four Customs officers at Ilfracombe, without arms or ammunition, and the nearest troops were fifty miles away.

After the Napoleonic War, Captain McCulloch instigated the Coastal Blockade, which recruited sailors who would otherwise have been pensioned off. They were known as The Warriors, and in 1818 were often quartered in Martello Towers. Their special role was to row in small boats close in-shore under the cliffs, surprise the smugglers while landing their cargo, seize the contraband and thus claim prize money. The smuggling vessel off-shore was left to the Revenue cutter.

On the whole the revenue officers did as good a job as they were able with few men and difficult terrain, but the odds were overwhelming. Apart from the specially built smuggling luggers, there were the Post Office packets and East Indiamen openly flaunting their defiance of the Customs in port, and even gentlemen's pleasure yachts slipping into little creeks and harbours with a cargo of contraband. A report in the *Exeter Flying Post* on 2nd February, 1832, describes how on the previous Saturday farmers had taken their horses down to the beach near Lynmouth and loaded them with thirty kegs of brandy from a vessel which lay off shore. They were interrupted by three preventive men; and the boat immediately set sail, putting in at Appledore. 'It was,' the report continues, 'apparently a pleasure yacht, the property of a gentleman of Appledore. Twenty-four kegs of spirit were seized.'

Sometimes the Customs blundered, as they certainly did at Bude on 15th January, 1831. Sighting a suspicious vessel, they gave chase, overhauled it, and went aboard. There they found a number of tubs, and, well-pleased with their catch, they seized the ship and brought her into Bude harbour. There they opened up the casks, only to find they contained nothing but salted herrings.

It was in 1822 that the Coast Guard came into being. It was paid for by the Customs, although it was also a Naval Reserve, which could be called up by the Admiralty as could the Coastguard cruisers.

Chapter 4

THE SMUGGLERS

WHAT were they like, these smugglers who appear to have dominated every aspect of our overseas trade for a century and a half? The popular view of a typical smuggler is a swashbuckling sea captain, running a gauntlet of Revenue cutters at sea and ambushes on shore to hide his contraband in secret caves in the cliffs. We have seen that there was much more to it than that. It involved four distinct groups of people; the venturer who put up the money, the captain and crew of the vessel that brought the contraband over the Channel, the overseas merchant who supplied the captain with the goods he required, and finally the organiser on shore who arranged for the landing, transportation from the shore, and distribution.

Sometimes these categories overlapped. A merchant might own his own ships, or a venturer might take a more active role than usual in the landing and distribution of the cargo. But on the whole the venturer, being a man of substance, had to remain anonymous, like the nameless baronet who hid contraband in his stables near Dartmouth. One of the very few names one finds in this category is that of Sir John Knill, Mayor of St Ives and Collector of Customs. He seems to have been behind all the considerable smuggling activities which went on in that port during his lifetime. Yet I doubt if he would be remembered by many today were it not for the fact that he built a folly and left a bequest that every fifth year, on 25th July, ten maidens and two matrons, accompanied by a fiddler, should dance around the monument, singing the hundredth psalm. It seems highly probable that the money for this bequest came from smuggling.

There is also the delightful story of Zephaniah Job, a poor school teacher of Polperro, who, in 1770, found that the local

Exmouth c.1840

fishermen wanted him to teach their children, but only sufficient arithmetic to convert pounds, shillings, and pence into francs and centimes, so they could keep their parents' smuggling account books straight. Realising that he could do this more accurately and quickly than his pupils, he set himself up as a smugglers' accountant. From that he progressed to become their agent, arranging supply contracts with the merchants across the Channel. For this service he charged no more than 1%, plus postage. Yet he amassed sufficient money to buy all the quays in Polperro; and eventually became a highly respected banker, albeit a smugglers' banker.

Perhaps I should have tried to find out more about Jack Corlyon of Coverack. He was a boat-builder who became a famous smuggler; a colourful character who always wore a red shirt about the village. When he went to sea he gave it to his wife to wash. On his return with a cargo of contraband, when he came in sight of land he first looked at the clothes-line, to see if his shirt was hanging out to dry. It was a signal that told him if the coast was clear.

From that picturesque company of West Country smugglers; 'Sweaty' Dunstan, 'Bobo' George, Richard Kingcup, Tom Crocker, 'Black Joan' and many, many more, I have chosen five to describe in detail. Each one involves others. One cannot deal with Isaac Gulliver without introducing John Fryer. Although Harry Carter wrote his autobiography, his brother, 'the King of Prussia', cannot be ignored. It was Captain Lancey who paid for Thomas Benson's crime. Rattenbury's activities involved the Mutters. And the mystery of 'Cruel' Copinger involves families whose descendants are alive today.

What I have tried to do in selecting these five characters is to cover the West Country geographically, and at the same time find representative examples of the different roles played by those involved in smuggling during the period under review. So one of them is a venturer and one an organizer representing the north and the south; two of them are sailors, one from Devon and one from Cornwall; the fifth, I believe, was a merchant who supplied smugglers as well as smuggling himself. He is also a legend linking north and south, Devon and Cornwall, and truth and fiction.

JACK RATTENBURY

JACK RATTENBURY was born at Beer, on the south coast of Devon in 1778, the son of a cobbler, who sadly never saw his son. He was taken away by a press gang while his wife was pregnant, and never seen again. At the age of nine Jack went fishing with his uncle, but, after losing the rudder, his tutor thought it better if he learnt fishing at someone else's expense. So he became an apprentice aboard a Brixham trawler for a while, and then a trading coaster. At this time he seems to have moved to successively larger vessels, so one is not surprised to find him deciding that privateering was really the life for him.

He was captured – and escaped. This happened with bewildering frequency throughout his life. Charm, subterfuge, force, prevarication, bribery, even good behaviour – Rattenbury used them all at one time or another to get himself out of a tight corner.

His memoirs were first published in 1837, and cover more than forty years of smuggling, privateering, and fishing, interspersed with piloting and even serving aboard a Revenue cutter which he tends to gloss over. As an author, he is seldom explicit when describing his smuggling activities. The only account of actually hiding contraband occurs as a footnote, which, in the 1967 edition of his memoirs, will be found on the penultimate page. It simply describes how a turkey was stuffed with lace instead of sage and onion, and a tin box, containing silk, was sealed with solder to make it water-tight. Cognac, gin, and tea were the main items of contraband that he brought into the country, though he did, on one occasion, unsuccessfully try to smuggle some French prisoners out of England.

He does not appear to have used Roscoff as a usual source of supply, preferring the Channel Islands and Cherbourg. He could

John Rattenbury, of Beer, Devonshire

get to Alderney and back to Beer in two days. The attempts made by the Customs to stamp out smuggling from Guernsey seem to have been singularly ineffective, judging by the number of fruitful runs that Rattenbury made.

One of the interesting points revealed in his book is the value of the hand-bill as evidence of good character. It seems to have served as a reference. When he saw a troopship standing into danger, he went aboard and, acting as pilot, brought the vessel to safety. The army officers, and no doubt the captain and crew, were extremely grateful; he was paid twenty guineas for his pilotage by the captain. As the officer commanding the troops seemed well disposed towards him, Rattenbury sought his advice. He explained that he had run into a bit of trouble with the Customs, and he wondered whether there was any way in which the rescue operation he had just completed could be turned to his advantage. The answer was to get a hand-bill printed describing how the ship, crew, and troops had all been saved; and the commanding officer gave him a guinea to defray the cost of printing. This hand-bill certainly had the desired effect with Lord Rolle, who on several occasions acted as Rattenbury's protector, and eventually allowed him a pension of a shilling a week.

One suspects that Lord Rolle's interest went deeper than sympathy for a smuggler. His family had, through marriage, come into possession of Bovey House, a fine Tudor mansion, standing a mile and a half north-west of Beer. It had been the home of the Walronds from 1300 to 1786, when Sarah, the last of the line, died. But the Rolles never lived there, and it remained empty for many years. Both the house and the lane leading to it were reputed to be haunted. It was, therefore, ideally suited to become a centre for smuggling. Although Rattenbury makes no mention of Bovey House by name in his book, perhaps because it was still being used as a hide for contraband when the book was written, Lord Rolle must have known full well what was going on. His family had always maintained a close interest in the village, and Lady Rolle endowed the almshouses and school in 1820.

Once, however, Rattenbury incurred his protector's displeasure. Rolle had given Rattenbury a letter of introduction to the Commander-in-Chief at Portsmouth, asking him if he could help in finding Jack some work. He was made, perhaps deliberately, a member of the crew of the Revenue cutter *Tartar*. Rattenbury says that he became ill and soon managed to gain his release, which made Lord Rolle very angry. But one wonders if he was really as angry as he appeared; for Rattenbury goes on, 'I afterwards called upon several gentlemen to whom I was known; and they each gave me a New Year's gift, which was the means of making myself and family very comfortable.' What did he tell these gentlemen? Perhaps he explained that he was not really a poacher turned game-keeper and was still prepared to continue to supply brandy, tea, and tobacco at extremely reasonable prices, should they so desire.

Although most of the runs he made were highly successful,

some failed and a number were downright dangerous. In 1812 the Revenue cutter *Catherine* fired twenty-four shots at his boat before catching up with him. On searching the vessel, no contraband was found, as Rattenbury had managed to sow the crop. Usually when this was done smugglers were able to retrieve the cargo within a few days. In 1815, however, Rattenbury was unable to use his creepers for three weeks, and during that time the weather was frosty. This ruined the contents of the tubs, making the spirit 'thick'.* Luckily for him such occurrences were rare. In October, 1816, he made seven trips; on four of these he 'did well', two were 'fairly successful' and only one was a failure, in this case because the kegs broke loose from their moorings in a gale.

A typical adventure is that which occurred in November, 1819. Returning from France, and within a league of the English coast between Lyme and Seaton, he sighted a suspicious sail. So he put his ship about and sailed eastwards. Unfortunately, the moon prevented him from studying the other vessel's movements, although his own were clearly visible. Half an hour later the strange ship had drawn sufficiently near for Rattenbury to recognise her as a Revenue cutter. He told his crew to get in the dinghy, but to hang on until he gave the word. He then put the helm hard over to send the lugger straight across the cutter's bows, shouted to his crew to shove off and leapt into the dinghy. While the Revenue cutter was luffing to avoid the lugger, Rattenbury and his crew managed to reach land, about a mile and a half from Beer, but leaving behind 300 kegs of spirit and several bales of tea. A few days later, he sent his wife to ask the captain of the Revenue cutter, then lying at Lyme, if he might have back the clothes that he had perforce left aboard his boat. The answer was, "Yes! If he comes and collects them himself!" This Rattenbury did, and was

---

*The origin of 'shrub' is said to be a cordial of herbs and spices specially blended to make smuggled spirits, especially rum, which had become tainted with sea-water, more palatable.

received 'most civilly'. One might have expected the captain to arrest him, but Rattenbury supposed that he must have been in a particularly good temper at capturing such a valuable prize.

One of his more famous escapes occurred when he and a companion, having stood trial at Falmouth, were sentenced to a term of imprisonment at Bodmin. Two constables were ordered to conduct them there, but Jack was determined to escape. In his memoirs he writes:

Accordingly when we came to the Indian Queen, a public house a few miles from Bodmin, while the constables were taking their potations I bribed the drivers not to interfere. Having finished, the constables ordered us again into the chaise, but we refused. A scuffle ensued. One of them collared me, some blows were exchanged, and he fired a pistol, the ball of which went off close to my head. My companion was engaged in encountering the other constable who called upon the drivers to assist, but they said it was their duty to attend to the horses. We soon got the upper hand... and seeing a cottage near, I ran towards it and the woman who occupied it was so kind as to show me through her house into the garden, and to point out the road. When I had proceeded about a mile, on looking back, I perceived a man following me... I crept into a ditch for concealment. When the person came up he hailed me by name, and I found it was my fellow prisoner... We went on our journey together, and towards evening, we met with a party of men who were smugglers like ourselves. They behaved very handsomely... and took us to a place called Newkey, where we slept. The next morning we got up very early and hired three horses for Mevagissey, the landlord going with us to take them back. Here we had the good fortune to fall in with a friend who lent us £10, our money being almost exhausted. We hired a boat which took us to Budleigh Salterton, that being the most convenient place to land as the wind was easterly. On the following day we walked on together and in the evening, to our great joy, arrived safe at Beer.

Jack Rattenbury did, however, spend some time in Exeter gaol. Here he received 22oz of bread every morning, and 10lbs of potatoes and 1lb of pork a week. He decided that he would rather have an allowance of 4½d. a day – and he got it.

Sometimes he found it expedient to travel as a passenger aboard someone else's ship, when travelling to France and bringing back a cargo. He would pay the owner or captain, who could be French or English, £25 a trip. Then if the vessel got caught he could plead that he had only booked a passage. On one such occasion the version that he gives does not quite tally with the official records. He apparently offered the master of the Lyme Packet, a man named Cawley, 12s. a cask for bringing back 227 casks from France. He 'and one of his partners' went as passengers to Cherbourg, where they took the cargo on board, and returned to England, making a landfall under Salcombe Hill fourteen hours later. At 1 a.m. Rattenbury and a boy left in the dinghy to get help in unloading. As they had not returned by dawn, Cawley became a little worried. He was still more perturbed when at 6.30 a.m. he saw that he was being watched by the Revenue cutter *Scourge*, commanded by Captain M'Lean. He tried to escape, throwing the contraband overboard as he went. The *Scourge's* boats were lowered and the tubs retrieved, while still giving chase to the Lyme Packet. Cawley was arrested and brought to trial at Exeter. There he implicated Rattenbury, who was still in hiding, and the partner, who was released on the grounds that he was only a passenger aboard Cawley's ship. Cawley and one member of his crew, however, were sent to gaol.

Rattenbury's version of the story is that
(a) the captain of the Lyme Packet was so drunk he allowed himself to be captured,
(b) he bribed his crew to give evidence against Rattenbury,
and (c) if his partner had been discharged without a stain on his character because he had been no more than a passenger then he, Rattenbury, was entitled to the same treatment. This cut no ice, and when he came out of hiding, a fortnight after 'this melancholy catastrophe', he was caught and his boat confiscated. 'By this means,' he writes, 'I was kept out of employment till the end of December, having no other boat to go to sea in, which was a great injury to myself and family.'

These memoirs were published while smuggling was still a lucrative business, which is no doubt why he gives few details of how and where he operated; and while he names officers in the Customs Service, the identity of his colleagues is not given. We do know, however, that one of his partners was Abraham Mutter of Harcombe. He was a turf and woodcutter. You will find Mutter's Moor still marked on the Ordinance Survey map, just west of Sidmouth. As he hawked his wares about the district with a horse and cart, he was extremely useful on the distribution side of Rattenbury's smuggling activities. Many a gentleman's house around Exmouth, Sidmouth, and even Exeter, received additions to their cellars and store-cupboards, as well as their woodsheds, from Abraham Mutter's cart.

His brother, Sam, was an excellent sailor, and when Rattenbury finally retired, it was he who took over the maritime operations, thus bringing the enterprise under one family. Salcombe Church was almost certainly used as a hide for contraband by the Mutters. In *The History of Salcombe Regis*, a manuscript by J. Y. Anderson-Morshead, a sexton called Robert Channon, who was born in 1803, is reported as saying that the Mutters were more artful than Rattenbury. He also said that when the Mutters kept a public house at Exmouth, the Customs officers learnt to look in for a pint whenever a run was suspected. If Mutter was not behind the bar, they knew their suspicions were confirmed and contraband was due to be landed on the next flood tide.

Abraham's son, John, also took part in the family business; but he was the last of the smugglers. His son, William, became a carpenter, post-master, and small-holder. And the next generation, too, looked to the land, farming near Ottery St Mary, where their descendants still farm today.

I think it must have been Mutter's cart that Rattenbury describes in his last smuggling venture:

In the beginning of the month of July, 1836, I went to Torquay in a cart, where we took in 20 tubs and proceeded in the same conveyance to Newton Bushel: but someone having obtained intelligence of the same, laid information against us, so that when we were about a mile out of Newton Bushel, at 10 o'clock at night, the officers came up on horseback, and one of them, taking hold of the reins of the horse, said, "I seize this horse and cart on behalf of the King and myself." Upon hearing this I directly made my escape, but the man to whom the cart belonged was taken into custody and conveyed to Exeter.

Thus ended my career as a smuggler...

How typical that it should have ended with yet another escape.

THE CARTERS OF PRUSSIA COVE

FRANCIS CARTER, born in 1712, was a Cornish miner; he also rented a small-holding for £12 a year at Pengersick, which lies between Helston and Marazion, just above Prah Sands. It is said that the family came originally from Shropshire, but the sons whom his wife Agnes bore made their name in Cornwall. Captain Harry (1749-1829); John, an elder brother; and Charles (1757-1833) were probably the most famous smugglers in the Duchy. Whether or not the other five brothers were so deeply involved is not known. In his *Autobiography of a Cornish Smuggler*, Captain Harry tells of his two elder brothers running contraband with him, and I think this must include Francis, who was born in 1745, though Thomas was also older. It was John who named the place from which they operated 'Prussia Cove'. As a child in the games he and his brothers played he always insisted on taking the role of the King of Prussia.

In his fascinating book, *Smuggling in Cornwall*, Cyril Noall points out that there are really three little inlets which were used in landing smuggled goods, Pisky's Cove, Bessie's Cove, named after Bessie Bussow, who kept a kiddlywink or beer shop on the cliffs, and Prussia Cove. Harry Carter refers to the King's Cove in his autobiography; and John B. Cornish, who edited the original manuscript in 1894, writes 'Porth Leah or King's Cove, now more usually known as Prussia Cove, lies a little to the east of Cudden Point. There are really two [inlets to the east of Pisky's Cove] divided from one another by a point and a small island called the Enez. The western one, generally called Bessie's Cove, is a most sheltered and secluded place... The eastern side of the point, where there is another small harbour, called the King's Cove, is more open.'

Penzance c. 1817

Captain Harry was a most extraordinary man. He was a staunch Methodist, and his religious fervour dominates his autobiography, which for pages on end, reads like an evangelical tract. He started his working life in the mines, but at the age of seventeen joined two of his older brothers at Porth Leah, where they spent their time in fishing and smuggling, sailing a small sloop of about ten tons. So successful was he that by 1774 he was able to have built a vessel nearly double the size, which, as he continued to prosper, he was soon able to exchange for a thirty-ton cutter, with a crew of ten. Harry was a strict disciplinarian and his men were forbidden to use bad language.

The Carters were always upright, God-fearing, and honest. When one of their contraband cargoes was seized by the revenue men and placed under lock and key at Penzance Customs House, John Carter organized a raid and retrieved his contraband, but the rest he left untouched. It would, he thought, be wrong to take anything which he did not consider rightfully his.

By 1777 Harry Carter was in command of a smuggling vessel of sixty tons, which was armed with sixteen carriage guns and carried a crew of thirty-six. Then he ran into bad luck. On his way to Guernsey to pick up a cargo of contraband he sprung his bowsprit and put into St Malo for repairs. As he had no proper ship's papers or customs clearance he was clapped into gaol on suspicion of being a pirate. At that time England was at war with America, and on 6th February, 1778, a treaty was signed between France and America. The French were loath to let Carter go, inspite of the documents which had been provided by his friends in Guernsey and Roscoff. It was only after his brother, John, had been able to persuade the authorities to organize an official exchange of prisoners that Harry was set free; even then he had to leave his fine ship behind.

On his return to Prussia Cove he took his smaller vessel on a run to South Wales. At that time a privateer called *Black Prince*, armed with sixteen guns and carrying a crew of sixty, had taken a number of ships as prizes. For some unknown reason Carter's little ship, half the size and carrying no more than ten men, was suspected of being this privateer, and the *Three Brothers* was ordered to capture Carter's vessel. Carter was on shore, arranging the disposal of his contraband, when the *Three Brothers* approached. The six members of his crew, whom Carter had left on board, cut their cable and ran, leaving Captain Harry on shore but taking his papers with them. It took his friends at Prussia Cove twelve weeks to clear him, 'through the Lords of the Admiralty'.

In spite of such set-backs, Harry Carter continued to prosper. He soon had a fifty-ton smuggling vessel armed with nineteen guns; and he writes, laconically, 'I went in her sometimes a-smuggling and had a great success. We had a new lugger built, which mounted twenty guns, and both went in company together from Guernsey a-smuggling along the coast, so that by this time I began to think something of myself again.'

It was while he was lying at Newlyn that he was requested to go in pursuit and apprehend the *Black Prince*. 'It was not,' he wrote, 'a very agreeable business.' Half-manned with a scratch crew, and in very heavy seas, he engaged his quarry in a running battle which lasted three or four hours. *Black Prince* got into difficulties and Carter asked the captain to abandon his ship. After a while, realising his position was hopeless, the *Black Prince's* captain stopped pumping and agreed to give himself up. However, as the crew of the *Black Prince* launched their boat, it filled with water, and Carter had to take his own boat to the rescue. He saved seventeen of the *Black Prince's* crew of thirty-one men, before the vessel sank.

On 19th April, 1780, Harry Carter married Elizabeth Flindel of Helford, and exactly one year later she bore him a daughter, who was given the same name as her mother. Yet there was no sign of him settling down; and in the middle of November he was again in trouble.

Running contraband into Cawsand, he brought his ship up to anchor, leaving the trisail, jib, and mizzen set. Seeing two rowing boats approaching he asked what they were, only to be told that they were coming to take off some of his cargo. They were, in fact, from a man-of-war, and they cut Carter's mizzen sheet, carried away the tack of the trisail with a musket shot, and swarmed aboard. In the hand-to-hand fight that ensured, Harry was slashed about the head with a sword. As he lay in the scuppers, dazed and bleeding, his crew were overcome and locked up below decks. Harry then heard two of the boarding party approach. "Here's one of the poor fellows, dead!" exclaimed one. "Put the man below," said his mate, but the first replied, "What's the use of putting a dead man below?"

By this time the vessel had run aground. Carter lay on his belly for two hours; then a sailor came up with a lantern and looked at him. He lifted a leg, and let it fall back on the deck. He slipped a hand inside Harry's shirt; "Why! He's as warm now as he was two hours ago! But his head is all to atoms!"

The vessel began to heel over on the ebbing tide, and this broke the painter of one of the man-of-war's boats, which began to drift away. Orders were given to man the second boat and pick up the first. In the confusion which followed Harry, with the greatest difficulty, just managed to struggle ashore. Here the smugglers half carried him into the village, where he found his brother. A doctor was called in, who discovered the bone in his nose had been slashed in two and he had two large wounds in his skull, from which several pieces of bone subsequently worked their way out. The following day the brothers took a chaise to Charles Carter's house. Harry's injuries were sufficiently serious for a doctor to accompany them as far as Lostwithiel. He spent a week with his brother; but on finding that there was a £300 reward being offered for his capture, he went into hiding first at 'a gentleman's house at Marazion for two or three weeks', and then at the farm at Acton Castle that his brother had rented. He alternated between these two places for some months. During this time he half-burnt his coal at night, so that it would not make smoke and so give his hiding place away. The doctor who attended him, it is said, was always blindfolded and led for the last mile of his journey. When his wounds were healed, he used to walk over to 'Prussia' in the evening to take a glass or two of grog with the Cove Boys.

In August 1788, he found that his wife had consumption, and he describes a sad parting they shared before he set sail in October, first for Leghorn and then New York, which he reached on 9th April, 1789. Four months later he learnt that his wife had died.

Although one of the main reasons for crossing the Atlantic must have been to avoid arrest, he seems to have enjoyed himself so much working for and with the Methodists in America that on coming home in October, 1790, he told his brothers that he thought he might return there.

They replied, "If you go to America we shall never see you no more. We are meaning to carry on a little trade in Roscoff, in the brandy and gin way, and if you will go there you will be as safe as in America. We will pay you for your commission – and you can carry on a little business yourself, if you should so please."

Captain Harry agreed, and on 19th April, 1791, he set sail in an open boat from the King's Cove and tied up in Roscoff fifteen hours later. The French Revolution was in full spate; on 21st June the French royal family were arrested at Varennes, but such events seemed to pass unnoticed by Harry Carter, though his own behaviour must have attracted quite a lot of attention amongst the local inhabitants. Apart from praying ten times a day, each forenoon and afternoon he would walk out along the cliffs and spend two hours singing hymns at the top of his voice, saying prayers and reading from the Bible. Yet the last thing he wanted to do was draw attention to himself. In fact he used unfrequented paths in order to avoid meeting anyone who might distract him from his communion with God. 'About this time,' he writes, 'I made myself a linen girdle to go about my loins, inside my shirt, and tied it tight. I thought I would be able to live on less food, and my spirit would become more vigorous in the ways of good… I found it quite disagreeable and so left it off.'

One Sunday in Roscoff he met the first captain he had served under, and they took a turn around the town. In the course of conversation Harry Carter commented on what a poor place it was for the public worship of God, adding that if he was back home in Cornwall he would be preaching. His companion replied, "Why don't you stand up here and say something to the people? All the English in the town would gladly hear you."

After much trepidation and consultation with his Maker, Captain Harry decided to give it a trial. He held a service on the quay, and between twenty and thirty Englishmen turned up. He continued to hold services every night when Englishmen were in port, for the following nine or ten months.

Once his family came over to see him, and once he returned to Cornwall for a short visit, but he was back in Roscoff by Christmas Day, 1792. Just over a month later, on 1st February, 1793, war was declared between England and France. The English merchants, sailors, and tavern keepers were technically prisoners of war, but they spent little time in gaol and for many their condition could be described as being under house arrest. In March Carter was sent to Morlaix, then back to Roscoff, only to return once more to Morlaix; this time in the company of Mr & Mrs McCulloch and Mr Clancie.

This is the first time that Carter mentions these famous smugglers' merchants. Clancie was closely connected with Copinger, as I describe in a later section. And although Carter does not mention Copinger (unless his occasional reference to Mr C. refers to Copinger rather than Clancie) he does spend some time with a third merchant, Mr Diot.

In August, 1793, they were given permission to return to England, and McCulloch bought a small boat in which to make the journey with his wife, two sons, a daughter, two maid-servants, a man-servant, Clancie, and Harry Carter. Just as they were about to leave the harbour they were again arrested. This turned out to be most fortunate as the boat was so rotten it could never have crossed the Channel.

Captain Carter spent a further eighteen months under house arrest. After the execution of Robespierre in July, 1794, a number of prisoners and suspects were pardoned, but it was not until six months later that Mr Diot was able to obtain a release for Clancie and Carter. On January 23rd, 1795, after three years a prisoner, Harry Carter was set free, though it was not until August that he managed to reach Cornwall. He spent some time with his brother John at Prussia Cove, his brother Charles at Keneggy, and with Francis at Rinsey. Here he decided to settle down; and for the next thirty years he spent his time tending a small-holding and preaching. He died on 19th April, 1829.

Meanwhile John Carter and the Cove Boys pursued their calling. His headquarters had been enlarged and even fortified. A story is told of how one day a smuggling lugger, chased by a Revenue cutter, sailed between the Enys and the cliffs. The Revenue men, not daring to follow under sail, lowered a boat to give chase under oars. John Carter thought they were coming rather too close to his base, and opened fire from his shore battery.

After John Carter, the family business was caried on by his son-in-law Captain Will Richards. An advertisement in the *Sherborne Mercury* for 9th May, 1803, for the sale of the lease of Prussia Cove gives a good idea of what the place was like. The Auction was announced to take place at the Star Inn, Marazion, on 24th May, 1803:

All those large and Commodious Cellars, Lofts, Salthouses, Fish-Presses, Boat-Beds, Capstan, good Dwelling House, and other conveniences and premises, situated at Port-leap [sic] Cove, otherwise Prussia's Cove, in Mount's Bay and in the parish of St Hillary... together with the said Cove and the Landing Places therein. The above premises are exceedingly well adapted and situated for carrying on any kind of trade or merchandise, as well as of the fisheries in Mount's Bay, and the fish of all kinds may be landed tythe-free. There is a mine adjoining, now working, for copper-ore, and a steam engine erecting thereon. The coals and other materials for the consumption of the said mine may be imported at the said cove. The said premises are now let to the under-tenants of Messrs John and Francis Carter, at the clear yearly rent of £87.

As Cyril Noall comments, 'perhaps the advertisement of the sale was a "blind", to try to convince the authorities that the family "business" was in the process of being wound up!' Certainly the Carters seem to have lived on after John Carter's death, for on 9th March, 1822, the death was announced 'on Monday last at Kings Cove, in Breage, of Mrs Carter, aged 84, relict of Mr Carter, who, during the time smuggling was at its height, was famed for his exploits, and well known by the title of the King of Prussia.'

THOMAS BENSON

WHEN John Benson, Bideford merchant of Knapp House, Northam, died in 1739, he left two sons, Peter and Thomas, and one daughter, Catherine, who married a man called Stafford. Thomas had married his first cousin, Frances Melhuish, two years previously. John, the eldest son, who lived at Parkham, had died in 1738, and Peter died in 1743. So Thomas inherited the family business, together with its fleet of ships, and Knapp House, which in all was said to have been worth £40,000. His main occupation at this time was trading with Canada, the American colonies, France, Portugal, and the Mediterranean countries. His fleet of more than a dozen ships brought back cod from Newfoundland, tobacco from Virginia and Maryland, and wine from Portugal. The firm exported woollen goods and coal, and it also manufactured rope. Amongst the ships which Thomas Benson owned was the only privateer based on the North Devon coast, the *Benson Galley*, armed with twenty guns.

Although in the eighteenth century there seems to have been little difference between a privateer and a pirate, their origins lay in opposing camps. A merchantman, set upon by pirates, would defend itself. If it was thought that the pirate had previously attacked and robbed another vessel belonging to the same owner, it was only reasonable to try to regain the stolen cargo. When we were at war and our enemy seized our ships, surely attack was the best means of defence? The Government recognised this and issued Letters of Marque, which were really no more than licences for merchant ships to attack enemy vessels and seize them as prizes. Ships and cargo were then brought home and sold. This continued well into the nineteenth century, as the advertisement columns in newspapers such as the *Exeter Flying Post* reveal.

Hillsborough, Ilfracombe, Devon
with Light House, from Capstone Parade

We, however, are concerned with the 1740s. Although the *Benson Galley* is said to have been the only privateer in Benson's fleet, other ships were armed and equally eager to engage the enemy, although they may not have been issued with Letters of Marque. *Britannia* attacked a Spanish ship and captured or killed eighty-four of the hundred-strong crew, without suffering any injury or loss. The oddest story concerns a vessel, armed with thirteen guns, called *Newkey*. She carried a crew of twelve, under the command of Captain Ley, seventy-one Irish passengers, and fifteen French prisoners. In November, 1744, she was attacked by a thirty-five- ton French privateer called *Pierre & Marie*, manned by Captain Jean Lacost of Morlaix and a crew of forty-seven. The Irish refused to fight, but two attempts to swarm aboard by the French were beaten back by the English, who were outnumbered by almost four to one. At the third attempt Captain Ley, who had a broken shoulder blade, surrendered. The casualties aboard *Newkey* were one of the crew and thirty-one of the Irish passengers dead, and another thirty wounded. Captain Lacost treated the English well, putting Captain Ley to bed in his own bunk, because he said they were brave fellows. The Irish he set adrift in the *Newkey*'s long boat to row to Ireland which lay about thirty-six miles away. One can only imagine that the success – or perhaps the celebration of this success – went to the French captain's head, because he became convinced that Hartland Point and Lundy were the French coast. When he realised his mistake, he promptly surrendered to Captain Ley, who brought the ship and both crews into Barnstaple.

Two years later, in 1746, Thomas Benson was made Sheriff of Devon, and within another twelve months he became the Whig Member of Parliament for Barnstaple. His business continued to prosper, and at that time more tobacco was brought from our colonies in Maryland and Virginia to Bideford than to any other port in England with the exception of London. Through his contacts in the capital he obtained the franchise for transporting convicts to our penal settlements in America. Convicts out and tobacco in would, he thought, make an admirable trading pattern. Perhaps this association of convicts and tobacco gave him the idea which led to his downfall; or maybe he simply became intoxicated by his success. In either case he conceived the idea of renting the island of Lundy from Lord Gower, and landing the convicts there to work for him. After all, his contract was to take them out of the country; and it could be argued that Lundy, twelve miles near enough off shore, was outside territorial waters... and while they were there, by Jove, they could construct a store for tobacco; tobacco on which duty had not been paid...

His ships could not, of course, arrive home from the colonies without the cargo set out on the Bills of Lading. So first they had to be cleared at Bideford or Barnstaple. By swearing that the tobacco was for export, it would be exempt from customs duty. The ships would then sail, ostensibly for a foreign port, but actually off-load the tobacco on Lundy where it would be stored in a cavern, which incidentally is known as Benson's Cave to this day. The convicts would help to unload the vessels, and carry the hogsheads up the cliff. They would then divide the contents into smaller packages, which could be more easily smuggled back onto the mainland, through little unwatched ports, such as Clovelly, or the remote coves along the coast.

After a time, unfortunately for Thomas Benson, the Customs became suspicious. In 1740, his ship *Grace*, under the command of Captain Hammett*, incurred Customs dues and penalties of £922 for the illegal importation of tobacco.

The following year two more of Benson's ships, *Nightingale* and *Britannia* were served with writs, which in themselves bear witness to the staggering scale of smuggling at that time. *Nightingale* was the subject of two writs: for £1,153 on 25,000 lbs of tobacco and £1,660 on another 36,000 lbs. No less than six writs related to *Britannia*, totalling £4,504 on 99,000 lbs of tobacco. Altogether Benson stood to forfeit £8,319; and, even worse, as a merchant, Sheriff and Member of Parliament, he would lose his reputation. He decided to fight the case, knowing that it would drag on, and hoping that something would turn up.

On 11th October, 1751, Benson's ship *Vine*, under the command of captain John Clibell, cleared the Customs at Barnstaple with sixty hogsheads of tobacco, bound for Morlaix, it was said. The ship put in at Milford Haven, supposedly waiting for orders. The Customs there became suspicious, and threatened to seize the ship and cargo; so *Vine* set sail. Three days later she was at Barry, ready to load coal. No ship could possibly have sailed from Milford to Morlaix, discharged her cargo, and returned to Barry in three days. The Customs visited Lundy, and found a number of staves from hogsheads and traces of tobacco. Things

---

*It would be interesting to know if Captain William Hammett was related to the Richard Hammett of Kennerland, to whom Zachary Hamlyn left his estate of Clovelly.

looked black indeed, and Benson decided on a last desperate scheme. *Nightingale* was getting old. He planned to insure her and her cargo, discharge this at Lundy, scuttle the ship – and claim the insurance.

In 1752 a party of Benson's friends visited Lundy and found convicts working there. They also learnt that a week or so before their arrival, eight had managed to escape in a boat to Hartland Quay. The stories that they could tell would greatly damage Benson's defence. He decided to put his plan into action.

According to the bill of lading, when Captain Lancey set sail from Barnstaple on Tuesday, 28th July, 1752, *Nightingale* was carrying 365 bushels of salt, 4 boxes of cutlery, 2 casks of haberdashery, 17 bales of broadcloth, stockings, duffles, kerseys and serges, 1 ton of nails, a hogshead of cordage, a box of lace and silks, 7 bales of Irish linen, and 6 hampers of wrought pewter. The crew consisted of John Lloyd, first mate; Anthony Metherall, second mate; James Bather, boatswain; Francis Shackstone and Richard Sinnett, seamen; John Sinnett, cook; and Thomas Sharpe and Thomas Husbands, ship's boys. Benson had himself chosen Lancey as Captain, and the Sinnetts. The rest had been recruited by an Appledore tailor called Thomas Powe, who was heard offering Bather 30s. a month to serve as boatswain aboard *Nightingale*. There was also a party of convicts on board; twelve male and three females – though Bather afterwards said there were thirteen males and one was left on Lundy. The men were shackled in pairs and the women manacled together.

By noon on Thursday they were off Lundy, having made slow progress in the light airs. The next day they discharged the cargo. According to Captain Lancey, they set sail again on at 8 a.m. on 1st August, but Bather later stated that they did not leave until Sunday, 2nd August. Be that as it may, *Nightingale* was set on fire and scuttled on Monday, 3rd August, fifty miles west of Lundy, and on Wednesday 5th August, the convicts and crew were landed at Clovelly.

Benson's luck appeared to have run out. In spite of swearing together with the captain and mates before the Public Notary that the fire on board *Nightingale* was an accident, Bather, the boatswain, talked too loudly in the taverns. Rumours came to the ears of Benson's rival in trade and bitterest enemy, Mathew Reeder, who persuaded Bather to turn informer. So the scuttling was brought to the attention of the authorities. While investigations were being made, the Customs won their case against Benson, who was ordered to pay £6,187. He made his fleet over to the Melhuishes, excepting the ships *Placentia* and *Peter*, for whom he had special orders. In December, 1754, he fled the country and settled in Portugal. There he was joined by his two remaining ships. *Peter* was sold, presumably to provide enough capital to continue trading with *Placentia*. He was joined in this venture by his nephew, Thomas Stafford.

In February, 1754, Captain Lancey, John Lloyd, first mate, and Powe, the tailor, were tried by the court of Admiralty at the Old Bailey. Powe had taken no part in the actual scuttling and so could not be tried along with the other two. He was, however, indicted for compounding a felony, and although this case never came to court, as Benson had escaped, he remained in gaol until 1758. John Lloyd was found not guilty and set free. John Lancey was found guilty, and on 7th June, 1754, was hanged at Execution Dock 'according to the Maritime Custom anciently used and observed'. That custom was for three tides to wash over the body of a hanged man.

Attempts were made by his sister and others to have Benson extradited, and he found it expedient to slip over into Spain until this blew over. He then returned to Oporto and he and his nephew continued successfully to trade.

In 1771, Thomas Benson, merchant, sometime Sheriff of Devon, once Member of Parliament for Barnstaple and smuggler, died peacefully in his bed...

Or did his conscience give him a twinge of remorse? I doubt it. To me Thomas Benson was a man who could not distinguish between right and wrong. He was completely amoral. It is strange that we hear nothing of his wife Frances or of his children, Peter, John, and Grace. One wonders why his nephew Thomas Stafford was singled out to join him, when Catherine Stafford tried to have him extradited. Perhaps his wife and his sister both disapproved of him so strongly that they would do anything to prevent their children from becoming involved in his affairs.

ISAAC GULLIVER

DURING the seventeenth and eighteenth centuries a number of rich merchants and men of property from London and elsewhere bought large tracts of land in Dorset, built houses and created estates, which were often further enlarged later under the Enclosure Acts. The Farquharsons, originally ship-owners in Aberdeen, came by way of London. The Beckfords had considerable interests in the West Indies, where William Beckford, twice Lord Mayor of London, was born. The sister of another Lord Mayor, Humphrey Parsons, married Sir Anthony Sturt, High Sheriff of Hampshire, who bought the Horton estate in Dorset in 1697. Their son, Humphrey, through his marriage to Diana Napier, also came into possession of Crichel and Brownsea Island, while their daughter married George Chafin of Chettle. Yet a third Lord Mayor of London had close connections with Dorset. This was Sir John Fryer, who was called in by Walpole to help clear up the South Sea Bubble scandal. His great-nephew, John Fryer, owned large areas of land between Poole and Christchurch, and his descendants together with John Tregonwell (whose family came from Cornwall) were responsible for the development of Bournemouth.

As a ship-owner and banker, John Fryer possessed the main assets of a merchant venturer. His large stretches of hinterland enabled him to help in the transportation of any goods which happened to be landed in out of the way places; and furthermore, as he was well-known to and liked by his neighbouring land-owners, he may well have been able to find customers for such goods. He was born in 1724 and married Anne Rolles, whose father was a rich merchant of Poole.

The role of the banker in smuggling has always been kept pretty

Budleigh Salterton, Devon.

dark, but it is extremely interesting to find in the admirable history of *Hartland Quay* by Michael Nix and Mark R. Myers, the local banker Edward Hockin, who died as recently as 1835, being concerned with smuggling. William Heard is quoted as remembering 'plenty of smuggling lodged all round (this) place.'

During the eighteenth century Poole did an enormous trade with Newfoundland. In 1788 the tonnage of shipping engaged in this business amounted to 6,000 tons, compared with the 3,000 tons which sailed out of Dartmouth. The trade was largely concerned with cod fishing, and of a total of 700,000 quintain of cod sent to European markets from Newfoundland, Poole ships carried 320,000 quintain, while Dartmouth accounted for 140,000. Other West Country ports supplied the rest.

Although this may seem rather far removed from smuggling, it was all of considerable interest to the man who came to be described in an official report of 1788 as 'the greatest and most notorious smuggler in the West Country in the tea and spirits trade.' His name was Isaac Charles Gulliver; and in John Fryer he saw the perfect venturer to back his enterprise.

Gulliver was born on 29th September, 1745, at the family farm which now bears his name at West Moors, Dorset. His father was one of the gang mentioned by an informer as having been involved in a fight with the Customs Service at Canford Cliffs. He was, therefore, presumably concerned with smuggling himself; probably, like so many farmers, in supplying transport.

Young Isaac was educated at Wimborne Grammar School, and at the age of twelve he is believed to have made several voyages, including one to the Channel Islands, in a privateer of 400 tons called *Dorset*. This vessel belonged to Humphrey Sturt, who made Brownsea Island, so strategically placed at the entrance to Poole harbour, his principal home. While still in his teens Gulliver sailed to Newfoundland, where he spent two summers and a winter. He had returned home by 1765, but whether or not he was involved in the skirmish with the Customs Service which led to the death of Robert Trotman that year, I do not know. This smuggler's grave in Kinson churchyard is marked by a stone bearing the following inscription:

> To the memory of Robert Trotman,
> Late of Road in the County of Wilts,
> Who was barbarously murdered on
> The shore near Poole, the 24th March, 1765.
>
> A little tea, one leaf I did not steal
> For guiltless Bloodshed I to God Appeal
> Put tea in one scale, human blood in t'other
> And think what t'is to slay a harmless brother.

I do not think that Trotman was a member of Gulliver's gang, because I doubt if this was yet organised, although I feel sure that, even at the age of nineteen, he had formed detailed plans for its creation, including the financial backing, and contacts for distribution (which John Fryer could provide), the transport (which his father and other farmers had at their disposal, as well as barns and out-houses in which contraband might be hidden), and even, perhaps, signalling stations. Brownsea Island was an obvious site for the latter; but Humphrey Sturt had also built an observatory, seven stories high, in red brick, near Horton, which still exists. It had the great advantage of being more than six miles inland, and therefore avoided suspicion. All that remained to complete his plans was the sea-faring side of the operation. Although Isaac Gulliver had some experience as a sailor, he seems to have been too busy, planning and organising, to spend much time at sea. Fortunately his brother had become an accomplished seaman.

Exactly when Gulliver made his first successful run is not known, but it was probably before 1769. In that year he married, at Sixpenny Handley, Elizabeth Beale, the twenty-eight year old daughter of a blacksmith, who also kept a public house at Thorney Down called the Blacksmith's Arms. In the early years of their marriage the couple took over the running of this inn, changing its name to the King's Arms. Situated on the main road from Blandford Forum to Salisbury, it made an excellent distribution point for contraband.

In 1777 their first child, Ann, was born, and two years later came a son, followed twelve months later by a second daughter, Elizabeth. Gulliver must have been well established as a smuggler by this time, because in 1776 he bought Eggardon Hill from the Reverend William Chafin of Chettle. This early British earthwork, eight miles west of Dorchester and about five miles from the coast, stands 820 feet above sea level, and for Isaac Gulliver it was another link in the chain of signalling stations he organised. Charles Warne's *Ancient Dorset*, published in 1856, contains this reference to Eggardon Hill: 'The small enclosure... was prepared for a plantation to serve as a local mark for certain vessels engaged in the contraband trade.'

Isaac Gulliver was himself becoming a man of property. Round about this time he owned or rented Howe Lodge at Kinson, North East Farm and Thickthorn Farm near Crichel, the family farm at West Moors, and High House, East End, Corfe Mullen. Howe Lodge in Brook Road has been demolished to make room for a housing estate. It contained secret passagers and a large cellar under the dining-room floor.

It seems probable that these properties were used for two main purposes: stabling the horses he used for transportation, and as caches in which contraband could be hidden pending distribution. Farms were particularly well suited for this purpose. An untethered bull with a notice warning interlopers of the beast's ferocity was a very effective method of keeping people away.

By now he had an extremely well organised gang of fifty to sixty men. They wore a livery of a smock and had their hair powdered. This earned them the nick-name of 'White Wigs'. Gulliver himself was known as 'The Gentle Smuggler', because members of his gang were forbidden to use fire-arms, or indeed any undue force, against the Customs Service. Gulliver's success came from using his wits, and he was a brilliant organiser. His territory ranged from Lyme Regis to Mudeford, the whole length of the Dorset coast; but his favourite landing places were the creeks around Poole and the chines found on the desolate stretch of coast to the east – where Bournemouth now stands – particularly Flag Chine. George Roberts, author of *A Social History of the South of England* and sometime mayor of Lyme Regis, describes how forty to fifty White Wigs would wait for the arrival of a smuggling lugger in a chamber at the mouth of Lyme river, taking refreshment and coolly passing the time away – less than a hundred yards from the Customs House. The Customs Collector at Poole considered Gulliver as 'a person of great speculatory genius' and indeed this is justified. It has been estimated that his smuggling ventures involved thirty ships, including his favourite *Dolphin*, which amongst them carried an annual cargo worth £20,000.

Of course, everyone knew what was going on; and there must have been many a wry smile on the faces of the readers of *The Salisbury and Winchester Journal* on Monday, 12th April, 1779, when they saw this advertisement: 'To be sold by auction by Robert Hart, at the White Hart in Longham, near Wimborne, on Monday the 12th April, between the hours of twelve and six in the afternoon, TWENTY GOOD PACKHORSES, the property of Isaac Gulliver, Esq, of the same place.'

Apart from farms, churches were often used as hiding places for contraband. On the walls of the church at Kinson, you can see where the stonework has been scored by ropes, when tubs were hauled up into the roof. Outside the porch there is a tomb which served as a cache. The church at Langton Matravers was also used by smugglers. But the Isle of Purbeck had one feature which was of particular use in running contraband: the quarries. Here are underground passages, chambers and caverns in bewildering profusion. Some were only known to the quarrymen, and they worked hand-in-glove with the smugglers. At Tilly Whim Caves and Dancing Ledge the stone face of the cliffs had been worked into what might almost be described as a smuggler's wharf. In his *Smuggler's Guide to Purbeck*, Clive R. Hardy tells the story of a large block of stone which lay for years at Durlston quarry. It was, the quarrymen said, of such poor quality that it was not worth selling. In fact, it was hollow: specially made to receive contraband.

If things were not always what they appeared to be, no more were people. Isaac Gulliver took great pleasure in disguise. Customs officers were once tipped off that the smuggler was to contact some of his gang at Wimborne market. Here the revenue men mingled with the crowd, peering at every suspicious face, but never realising that the old, grey-haired shepherd, who had come in early with his sheep, was none other than Isaac Gulliver. It must have given him particular pleasure to don the very uniform his own gang always wore, smock and powdered hair, and still elude his pursuers.

Legends are often attributed to others beside the originator, and the story of the smuggler who feigned death to escape the Revenue men is no exception. Whether it was 'Resurrection' Jackman or 'The Gentle Smuggler' who first fooled the authorities in this way does not really matter. It was probably used on several occasions by different smugglers. The Gulliver version tells how he was chased by Customs officers right up to the door of his house, which he just managed to slam shut and bolt in their faces. They hammered to be let in, but Gulliver refused, knowing they could not produce a warrant. By the time one had been obtained, several days had elapsed. When they again knocked at the door of Gulliver's house, which had been kept under surveillance to ensure that he did not escape, they were greeted by a tearful Mrs Gulliver, who told them that it was too late; her husband had died. She bade them come in and pay their last respects to their old enemy, who, after all, had done them no harm. The Revenue officers went in and found an ashen-grey corpse with pennies on his eyes, lying in a coffin. They removed their hats, muttered a few condolences and tiptoed out of the house. Gulliver jumped up and promptly filled the coffin with contraband, ready for the hearse to take away.

Everyone, except perhaps the Customs service, was full of admiration for such an ingenious and successful character; a man, moreover, who had a keen sense of humour and a stylish appreciation of the good things in life. He was a wine merchant as well as a smuggler, and he was always careful to see that a modicum of his stock passed through Customs and that duty was paid on it. The local gentry, sipping their smuggled spirits, could truthfully tell their guests that such excellent brandy could be obtained from the wine merchant in Poole.

John Fryer was of great assistance not only in providing finance and introducing potential clients, but in helping him to establish a social position, particularly after his younger daughter, Elizabeth, married Fryer's eldest son, William. In 1797 this couple were blessed with twin sons, the first of seven children, most of whom were equally prolific, for William and Elizabeth had forty grand-children. Among their descendants one finds Lt General Sir John Fryer, KCB and Sir Frederick Fryer, KCSI, Governor of Burma. Fryer's bank also prospered, spreading out from Wimborne with branches in Poole, Wareham, and Blandford, before amalgamating with the National Provincial. Amongst its clients was the exiled King of France.

Gulliver's other daughter was not so fortunate. Her husband

turned out to be a drunkard, who made her life a misery. She was eventually rescued by her brother, young Isaac. This led to her husband having the following hand-bill printed:

ELOPEMENT
Southampton, June 6th, 1797.

Whereas Ann, the wife of Edmond Wagg, Esquire, of Whiteshead's Wood, near Southampton, did, on Saturday night last, elope from his dwelling-house with her brother, Isaac Gulliver, having taken with her all the plate and linen belonging to the said Edmond Wagg; this is therefore to give notice that the said Edmond Wagg will not be accountable for any debts whatsoever that his wife may contract from this day.

The plate and linen, needless to say, were a part of her dowry. Fortunately perhaps, Wagg died less than two years later, aged twenty-four. Sadly, Isaac Gulliver's only son died at the same age in 1798, from a chill caught from sleeping in damp sheets at Sherborne. On a happier note, Ann subsequently married a widower, Dr Andrew Crawford, with whom she found great happiness.

To Gulliver, consolidation of his standing must have come with the King's pardon. The story which has been handed down in the family is that he or one of his gang, on a trip to France, got wind of a plot to assassinate George III. The King happened to be at Weymouth at the time, and Gulliver sought an audience and was able to warn him. As a sign of his gratitude, the King pardoned Gulliver for any illegal activities in which he might have been engaged. There is another version, to which no doubt the Customs Service subscribed. This suggests that he took advantage of the law which allowed a smuggler to be pardoned if he were to serve in the Royal Navy *or find two other able-bodied men to take his place.*

I prefer the first story, not merely because it is more colourful and in keeping with the character of the man, but because smugglers in those days were very often concerned with espionage. As one of his descendants told me, "Isaac Gulliver was certainly a much more successful British agent than the ordinary spy. He always knew exactly where the French fleet lay; and often much more than just that."

Gulliver's greatest adversary was undoubtedly William Arnold, Customs Collector on the Isle of Wight. His father had been Collector of Excise at Poole, and his son became the famous headmaster at Rugby. In October 1783, he reported a new development in smuggling, and one which was doubtless pursued by Gulliver. He informed the Customs Board in London that smuggling was then being carried out by large armed luggers of 200 – 300 tons, (old measurement) from which contraband was landed in open day, under the noses of the Revenue cutters. 'Their masters,' he wrote, 'took out commissions as privateers, though they followed no other trade than smuggling. Now the war is over they continue their illicit practices.'

When a smuggling vessel was chased by a Revenue cutter, as often as not the Customs officers would see a small boat quickly lowered and rowed in haste towards the shore. If the Revenue cutter followed this boat they would find no contraband, for this was still on board the lugger which, in the meantime, had made its escape.

The Customs Service in Dorset had a particularly difficult time. When Gulliver's smuggling activities were at their height, a Riding Officer's pay was twenty pounds a year, plus a percentage of the value of captured contraband. Smugglers themselves were rarely apprehended. It was simply not worth while, as the magistrates were always excessively lenient. Customs officers knew that Gulliver's gentle smugglers would not attack, but they might well defend themselves if any attempt was made to arrest them. Furthermore by letting smugglers escape the Customs officers often augmented their income. Gulliver was generous; and the extent to which the Customs service at Pool worked with him can be seen from the following report from William Arnold.

Amongst the papers found on board the smuggling vessel brought in by the *Wasp*, sloop-of-war, was the enclosed letter from Mr Weston to John Early – a smuggler of great notoriety and property, giving an account of the Military force stationed at Poole. The very strong similitude between the writing of the name Weston in the letter and the signature of the Comptroller of Poole leads me to apprehend that he may well have been so imprudent as to give intelligence to Early of the soldiers quartered there to act against smugglers. We hope that Mr Weston may satisfy you that it is not his handwriting.

Apparently Mr Weston was not able to give a satisfactory answer, and two months later he was dismissed from the Service. How useful information on military matters would have been is extremely debatable. Time and time again did the Riding Officer at Poole request the support of the Light Dragoons, and on each occasion some excuse was made for not helping the Customs. Gulliver saw that the regimental mess at Wareham barracks was well supplied.

Things got to such a pass that on 17th October, 1806, the Poole Riding Officer in his request for support stated that 'the smugglers have got so impudent that they will not give up any quantity of goods except that an officer has military assistance with him.'

Soon after this Isaac decided to retire. The last years of his life were spent in West Boro, Wimborne, on the opposite side of the street to the Fryers who had given him such support. They lived in what are now numbers 64 and 65, while the counting house was number 72. Isaac Gulliver, church warden, devoted father, loving husband and, perhaps uniquely, honourable and gentle smuggler, died on Friday, 13th September, 1822, leaving £60,000. His memorial, rather worn today, is set in the floor of the nave in Wimborne Minster.

CRUEL COPINGER

SO FAR we have described the lives of two sea-going smugglers, Jack Rattenbury and Harry Carter, two shore based organisers, Thomas Benson and Isaac Gulliver, and introduced the typical venturer in John Fryer and distributor in Abraham Mutter. Their stories are factual. In Cruel Copinger we are faced with a legend; but a legend which, from time to time, tantalisingly reveals glimpses of actual events. It would take a lifetime to sift the facts from the fiction and fill in the gaps. So for the moment I propose to set out the legend, and then present all the evidence I have been able to muster to confirm or disprove it, and suggest a possible explantion for the conflicting stories.

The legend would make a splendid strip cartoon or scenario for a horror film. Imagine, then, a remote cove on the north coast, close to the Devon and Cornish border, backed by towering cliffs, and flanked by ridges of ragged rock running out to the sea that stretches westward without a break across the Atlantic to Labrador; a vast expanse that builds up mountainous waves which thunder onto the shore. It is a wild, stormy night, and in the occasional flash of lightning the little group of people at the water's edge see a ship with broken mast and tattered sails standing in towards them. The group contains many who are praying for a wreck, men who are anxious to plunder whatever cargo the ship may carry. But there are also two women in the crowd, a girl, Dinah Hamlyn, riding a grey horse, and an old beldam in a red cloak. As the listing vessel approaches, they see a tall, fierce figure standing in the prow. It is John, alias Cruel, Copinger, the Dane.

Stripping off his shirt and breeches he leaps ashore, seizes the cloak from the old beldam, and leaps to the crupper of Dinah's horse. They gallop off into the night.

John Copinger ats Cruel Copinger
B. 30 Sept. 1723.

From a portrait reproduced in the Western Antiquary of 1893.

Dinah Hamlyn lives at Galsham, and here her father and mother make Cruel Copinger welcome. He, finding that Dinah is an heiress, proposes marriage, hinting that the farm should be the dowry. Hamlyn on his death bed implores Copinger to look after his wife and daughter, gives him his blessing and dies.

Copinger becomes a smuggler, sailing his ship the *Black Prince* over to France and bringing back brandy, lace, and tea. He is also a privateer, though he holds no Letter of Marque, capturing as prizes many innocent craft. Chased by the Customs Service, he slashes an officer's head off with one blow of his sword. Back in his cave six miles south of Hartland Point at Gull Rock, 'as big as Kilkhampton church' he celebrates his escape with a wild carousel. The food comes from the sheep and cattle he has stolen. The drink consists of the brandy, gin, port, and sherry he has smuggled. The doxies are dressed in little but the lace and silk he has also brought over from France.

On this occasion his wife, needless to say, remains with her mother at Galsham. She is about to have Cruel Copinger's child. This turns out to be a deaf mute. He grows up to be a little brute, throwing his playmate over the cliff and smiling happily at the broken body on the rocks below.

When Customs officers visit Galsham, Copinger tells his wife to hide the smuggled silk and lace in the oven while he shows them some empty brandy casks. When the Customs have left Copinger is furious to find the silk and lace is scorched. He ties Dinah to the bedpost and tells her mother that he will flay her daughter alive unless she hands over all her jewels. On his way to his cache in Herstridge Wood, where he has decided to hide the jewels, he meets the vicar of Stratton, who asks him for his tythes. Copinger belabours the parson with his whip, cutting him about the face and head. "There's your damned tythes," he shouts, "And I'll not ask for a receipt!"

And so he went on, smuggling, privateering, whipping those who dared to ask for their money, beating his wife, drinking, swearing, whoring and so on, and so on, until one day a ship stood into a cove, Cruel Copinger leapt aboard and was never seen again. But a mighty storm arose, the trees around Galsham were uprooted and a thunderbolt crashed through the roof, landing on the chair where Copinger usually sat...

> Would you hear of 'cruel' Copinger
> He came from a foreign kind;
> He was brought by the salt water,
> And was taken away by the wind.

This brief account has been pieced together from the many legends that have been told about John Copinger. There are others, but let this suffice.

What are the facts?

A man called Copinger is said to have been wrecked at Marsland Mouth on 23rd December, 1792. His name was Daniel Herbert Copinger, not John. But the evidence is not conclusive. It is based on a window pane which carried these words scratched with a diamond. 'D. H. Coppinger, shipwrecked 23rd December, 1792; kindly received by Mr Wm Arthur.' Golden Park, the farm where William Arthur lived is much nearer Marsland Mouth than Galsham, but a pane of glass which bears Copinger's signature, though not the message, is still to be seen at the latter place. Copinger could have scratched both panes, one of them, or none.

Daniel Herbert Copinger, not John, did marry Miss Hamlyn of Galsham, but her name was Ann not Dinah, and she was hardly a young girl. She was the forty-two year old daughter of Acland Hamlyn. The proof of this lies in the Marriage Certificate now in the County Record Office in Exeter, which confirms that Daniel Herbert Copinger, of the King's Royal Navy, married Ann Hamlyn, aged forty-two on the 3rd day of August, 1793, at Hartland Parish Church. But there is no record of a Copinger in the Navy List around that date, nor of a naval vessel being wrecked at Marsland Mouth.

As we have seen in the life of Harry Carter,there was a privateer called *Black Prince*, capturing prizes at that time, and this was said to be manned largely by Irish. According to the Copinger family tree the family had lived in Ireland for at least eight generations by the end of the eighteenth century. Yet Michael Copinger in a letter dated 12th November, 1981, informed me that the name was originally Copyner, which was Danish. There is further evidence of the privateering activities of the *Black Prince* in *Wreckers and Wrestlers* by Roger Parnall. On 23rd July, 1779, the Brig *Union* from Boscastle to Bristol, John Trick, Master, was taken off the coast of St Genny's (on the north coast of Cornwall, a few miles south west of Marsland Mouth) by an armed vessel, cutter rigged, the master of which said she was American, the *Black Prince* from Boston. The brig was ransomed for £200. Carter said the *Black Prince* was from Dunkirk, but the names of vessels and their ports of origin were often changed to avoid capture.

We can trace Daniel Herbert Copinger's history a little further. He was made bankrupt in 1802 and imprisoned in the King's Bench Gaol. On his release he lived in Barnstaple on an allowance from his estranged wife. She survived him, for she is described as a widow on her death certificate. She died on 31st August, 1833, and lies buried next to her mother in Hartland Church. In her will she left property in Port Isaac and St Neot. Michael Copinger remembers seeing a cottage called Copinger's at Port Isaac. There is also a Copinger's Cave in that area, and a tradition that he operated around Pentire Point, making Pentire Glaze his headquarters.

Was Daniel Herbert Copinger a naval officer or a smuggler? A bankrupt failure, living on an allowance from his wife or a swashbuckling villain? I do not think that Daniel Herbert could have been Cruel Copinger.

In the Copinger family tree one finds three members of the family outlawed for High Treason. Thomas Copinger in 1641, Walter Copinger in 1694, and his son James. Furthermore, S. Baring Gould in the *Western Antiquary* quotes Dr Donavan, who in his sketches of Carbery describes a Sir Walter Copinger living in 1608, in the following words: 'During his residence at Newry he was chiefly distinguished by his tyrannical qualities. No Russian nobleman of former times lorded it over his serfs with such despotic sway... It is related how he had a yard-arm extended from one of the gable ends of the mansion... [known as Copinger's folly and the largest house in Carbery] which served the purpose of a gallows wherewith to hang the victims of his unlicensed power. Stories are also told of a dark dungeon beneath the basement storey of the Court, where prisoners pined for years in wretchedness and chains.'

It is S. Baring Gould's contention that Cruel Copinger was John Copinger whose father he says was also outlawed for high treason. He left Ireland first for Cornwall, then he spent a period in Roscoff before returning to Cornwall and settling at Trewhiddle near St Austell.

We have seen in the chapter on organisation that John Copinger was a highly successful merchant of Roscoff supplying no less than 3,783,909 lbs of tea and 19,400 hogsheads of brandy to the smugglers over a period of ten years, and that Copinger, Clancie, and Company were taxed in 1785 at £260 compared with McCulloch who was taxed at £48 and Diot & Company at £24. He was, therefore, probably the biggest of the smugglers' suppliers. He may well have sailed his own fleet of ships and indulged in smuggling himself. S. Baring Gould says 'John Copinger was undoubtedly employed by the English government on secret services during the war with France, and he owned his own schooner in which he went to and returned from the French coast, with communications to and from agents in France.'

It is said that he lost his Roscoff property during the French Revolution, and Michael Copinger told me that his great-great-grandfather, who was John's eldest son, James George, went over to France during the Revolution to get his younger brother and sister out of the country and bring them back to Trewhiddle. He was arrested as an aristocrat, and had his hair cut short in preparation for the guillotine he had to face the following dawn. That very day news came through that following Robespierre's execution prisoners were to be released, as I have already mentioned in the story of Harry Carter. Captain Harry must have been in Roscoff at the same time as James Copinger.

It struck me as strange that such an important merchant does not figure in Carter's autobiography. Lesser names such as

McCulloch and Diot occur, but not Copinger. I believe that I found the reason in *Le Port et Havre de Roscoff*. Here Professor Jean-Yves Tanguy states that 'the house of Copinger and Company was known under the name of Clausic.' after studying some of the documents on which this is based, I have come to the conclusion that the Professor has misread the name, turning an n and a c into a u and an s which do look very similar. The name under which Copinger operated should be Clancie not Clausic, and Clancie is indeed mentioned by Carter.

Not only is there a lack of any direct reference to Copinger's Roscoff activities in any English source of smuggling information but there is even a scarcity of factual information about his life in Cornwall. He is said to have settled at Trewhiddle, and I believe this to be true, although I have not yet found any documentary evidence. Yet here again there is a clue which might lead to confirmation. Trewhiddle, which, like Benson's Knapp House, is now a holiday park, was for many years associated with the Polkinhorne family; and John Copinger's grand-daughter, who was born on 12th August, 1814, at St Austell, was christened Ann Frances Polkinhorne, although the family tree reveals no Polkinhorne connections.

The family maintained extensive connections with Brittany in spite of the Revolution, in which John is said to have lost his Roscoff property. James George is described as being 'of Roscoff' and his son James Erhart Copinger lived at the Chateau du Bec de la Vallée Dinard, near St Malo; Another son served in the French Army, while two daughters died in France and John's daughter Barbara married a Monsieur de Caix.

John Copinger was certainly a highly successful smuggler's merchant and may well have indulged in smuggling himself; he was most probably deeply involved in the Secret Service, and acted as a British agent, but was he, as Baring Gould suggests, the Cruel Copinger of legend? It seems extremely unlikely that John Copinger, whose daughters married into highly respectable families and two of whose sons served in the Royal Navy, should have perpetrated half the crimes attributed to Copinger the Dane.

May it not be possible that his secret work for the British Government was considerably more important than has ever been revealed? In this case, is it beyond the bounds of possibility that he deliberately resuscitated the stories of cruelty attributed to his ancestor and adopted them as his own, to provide a reason for his movements perhaps, and, at the same time, frighten God-fearing countryfolk away from such a monster? In all probability the stories lost nothing in the telling, as Copinger well knew. In the legend Copinger is always described as a Dane, and this is particularly interesting as although the family had been in Ireland since 1550 and probably were there before the Norman Conquest, there is a family tradition that they originally came from Denmark.

There is a theory which I have discussed elsewhere, that the legend of the Cannibals of Clovelly was deliberately given publicity to keep inquisitive young eyes away from caves containing contraband. The legend of Cruel Copinger may have similar origins.

Be that as it may, there still remains this question: who was Daniel Herbert Copinger, who married Ann Hamlyn? Although John Copinger had a son called Daniel Laurent, according to the family tree he married Emily, the daughter of Sir John Murray, Bart, of Peebles. There are, however, several other branches which could well have borne fruit, though none is recorded. John's brother Thomas, who died in Lisbon, might have married and produced a son. So might John's uncle, Walter. Going further back, James who was outlawed for treason and went to France, where he was living in 1700, might also have been a forbear of Daniel Herbert.

The story of Cruel Copinger still poses more questions than it answers.

*   *   *   *

The best unsolicited testimonial any smuggler could wish to have comes from a Naval officer. In his *History of the Royal Navy* Captain Brenton, R N writes:

These men are as remarkable for their skill in seamanship as for their audacity in the hour of danger; their knowledge has been highly advantageous to the Navy, into which, however, they rarely enter unless sent on ships of war as a punishment for some crime committed against the Revenue Laws. They are hardy, sober, faithful to each other beyond the generality of seamen; and when shipwreck occurs, have been known to perform deeds not exceeded in any country in the world, probably unequalled in the annals of other maritime powers.

The Royal Navy found smugglers much better seamen than the usual run of men rounded up by the Press Gangs and they gained rapid promotion.

Barnstaple, 1836

Chapter 5

BALLADS

WHEN describing past events, one of the most difficult things for an author to establish – and a reader to appreciate – is the true historical reaction. It is all too easy to judge yeserday's actions in the light of today's customs and belief. Wherever possible I have quoted contemporary reports *verbatim*. But although these may provide the right period flavour, they are more likely to reflect an official viewpoint than popular feeling. It struck me that Broadsheets of the period might well provide the latter. Thanks to Tish Stubbs I am able to add three broadsheets, and a song she collected from a Norfolk singer in 1977, for which I am particularly grateful.

THE SMUGGLER KING

London: — H. Such, Printer and Publisher, 177, Union Street, Boro.'

There's a brave little bark, stealing out in the dark,
From her nest in the bustling bay;
The fresh breeze meets the dingy sheets,
And swiftly she darts away.
She never must run in the eyes of the sun,
But along with the owl take wing;
She must keep her flight from the moon-lit night,
For she carries the smuggler king!

She must, &c.

A monarch is he, as bold as can be,
Of a strong and daring band;
The bullet and blast may go whistling past,
But he quails neither heart nor hand;
He lives and dies with his fearful prize,
Like a hunted wolf he'll spring,
With trigger and dirk, to the deadliest work,
And fight like a smuggler king.

Back from the wave to our home in the cave,
By the gleam of our torches glare,
He reigns as lord of the freebooters' board,
And never was costlier fare.
Right firm and true are the hearts of his crew,

And there's faith in the shouts that ring,
As they stave the cask, and drain the flask,
In a health to the smuggler king.

WILL WATCH
THE BOLD
SMUGGLER

J. Catnach, Printer, 2, Monmouth-court, 7 Dials.
Cards Printed very Cheap.
Sold by Bennett, Brighton & Pierce, Southborough.

Twas one morn when the winds from the northward blew keen,
And fullenly roar'd the big waves of the main;
A famed smuggler, Will Watch, kifs'd his Sue then ferenely,
Took helm and to fea, boldly fteer'd out again.
Will had promif'd his Sue that this trip if well ended,
Should coil up his hopes, and he'd anchor on fhore,
When his pokets were lined, why his life fhould be mended,
The laws he had broken he'd never break more.
His fea boat was trim, made her port took her lading,
Then Will ftood for home reach'd the offing &c.
This night if I've luck furls the fails of my trading
In dock I can lay, ferve a friend too befide.
Will lay too till night came on darkfome and dreary,
To crowd every fail, then he pip'd up all hands,
But a fignal foon fpied 'twas a profpect uncheerly,
A fignal that warn'd him to bear from the land.

The Philiftines are out, cries Will, we'll take no heed on't
Attack'd, who's the man that will flinch from his gun
Should my head be blown off I shall ne'r feel the need on't

We'll fight while we can, when we can't boys we'll run,
Through the haze of the night a bright flash now appearing,
O ho! cries Will Watch the Philiftines bear down,
Bear a hand my right lads e'er ye think about sheering,
One broadfide pour in should we fwim boys or drown.

But should I be pop'd off you my mates left behind me,
Regard my last words fee them kindly obeyed,
Let no ftone mark the fpot, and my friends do you mind me,
Near the beach is the grave where Will Watch would be laid,
Poor Will's yarn was fpun out, for a bullet next minute,
Laid him low on the deck and he never fpoke more,
His bold crew fought the brig, while a fhot remain'd in it,
Then sheer'd and Will's hulk to his Sufan they bore.

In the dead of the night his last wish was complied with,
To few known this grave, and to few known his end,
He was borne to the earth by the crew that he died with,
He'd the prayers of his Sufan the tears of his friends.
Near his grave dash the billows the winds loudly bellow.
Yon ash ftruck with lightning points out the cold bed,
Where Will Watch the bold fmuggler, that dammed lawless fellow,
Once fear'd now forgot fleeps in peace with the dead.

THE POOR SMUGGLERS BOY

One cloudy cold morning abroad I did steer
By the wide rolling ocean so deep and so fair
I met a poor boy who in sorrow did weep:
Alas my poor father was lost in the deep.

Mast, sails and rigging all sunk in the wave
And found with poor father a watery grave.
I jumped from the wreck and clasped him to me
But his form, it was lifeless, sank into the sea.

I clung to a plank and swam for the shore
Bad news for poor mother, dear father no more.
She died broken hearted, nor heeded the moan
Of the poor smugglers boy left to wander alone.

A fine wealthy lady who heard him complain
Took him in for shelter from the cold and the rain.
I will care for this orphan till the day that I die
No more will he wander with his sad lonely cry.

The lady did die, he the master became
She left everything in her will to his name
And she kept her promise till the day she did die
To care for the orphan with his sad lonely cry.

Poor father did venture all on the salt sea
With a cask of good whiskey to the land of the free
The lightning did flash and the thunder did roar
Our ship it was wrecked while far off from the shore.

O pity I crave won't you give me employ
Alone I must wander, cried the poor smuggler's boy.

THE FEMALE SMUGGLER

Come list awhile, and you soon shall hear,
By the rolling sea lived a maiden fair,
Her father followed the smuggling trade,
Like a warlike hero that never was afraid.

In sailor's clothing young Jane did go,
Dress'd like a sailor from top to toe,
Her aged father was the only care,
Of the Female Smuggler, who never did despair.

With her pistols loaded she went on board,
By her side hung a glittering sword,
In her belt two daggers – well arm'd for war,
Was the Female Smuggler, who never fear'd a scar.

Not far they sailed from the land,
When a strange sail put them all to a stand,
Those are sea robbers, this maid did cry,
The Female Smuggler will conquer or die.

Close along-side these two vessels came,
Cheer up said Jane, we'll board the same,
We'll run all chances to rise or fall,
Cried the Female Smuggler, who never feared a ball.

They beat the robbers and took their store
And soon returned to old England's shore,
With a keg of brandy she walked along,
Did the Female Smuggler, and sweetly sung a song.

Not far she travelled before she espied
A Commodore of the blockade,
He said – surrender! or you must fall.
But the Female Smuggler said, I never feared a ball.

What do you mean? said the Commodore,
I mean to fight, for my father's poor,
Then she pulled the trigger and shot him through,
Did the Female Smuggler, and to her father flew.

But she was followed by the blockade,
In irons strong they put this fair maid,
But when they brought her to be tried,
The young Female Smuggler stood dress'd like a bride.

The Commodore against her appeared,
His health restored, and from danger cleared,
But when he found to his great surprise,
'Twas a Female Smuggler had fought him in disguise –

He to the Judge and Jury said,
My heart won't let me prosecute that maid,
Pardon I beg for her on my knees,
She's a valiant maiden, so pardon if you please.

If you pardon this maid, said the gentleman,
To make her my bride now is my plan,
Then I'd be happy for evermore,
With my Female Smuggler, said the bold Commodore.

Then the Commodore to her father went,
Though he was poor, to ask his consent,
He gained consent, so the Commodore,
and the Female Smuggler are joined for evermore.

Chapter 6

PLACES

Including Inns and Taverns Connected with Smuggling

THERE is hardly a cave or cove, creek or beach, in the West Country that has not been the site of some smuggling activity. Here is a gazetteer of the most famous places which you can visit but not arranged alphabetically. The names are arranged in a geographical sequence following a route which leads down the Bristol Channel, west to Cape Cornwall and Land's End before turning eastward along the south coast of the peninsula, thus covering the shores of Somerset, Devon, Cornwall, and Dorset. Where a description of the place is to be found in the text, the page reference is given to avoid unnecessary repetition.

1 *Middle Hope.* Woodspring Bay and the coast from St Thomas's Head to Sand Point was a favourite place for landing contraband.

2 *Worle Church.* See page 24.

3 *Uphill Church.* See page 24.

4 *Flat Holme.* See page 3.

5 *Kilve and St Audries' Bay.* This was another strip of coast much favoured by smugglers when bringing their cargoes ashore.

6 *Lynmouth.* The Rising Sun is an old smuggling tavern. At one time donkeys were kept here, like those at Clovelly, to carry half-ankers of spirit, bales of silk, and packages of tea up onto Exmoor. Page 34.

7 *Smuggler's Leap.* Just above Lee Bay there is a chasm where a smuggler, chased by a revenue officer, both on horseback, dragged his pursuer over the cliff. Nearby there are caves in which contraband was once hidden.

8 *Heddon Mouth.* Another favourite landing place; but one

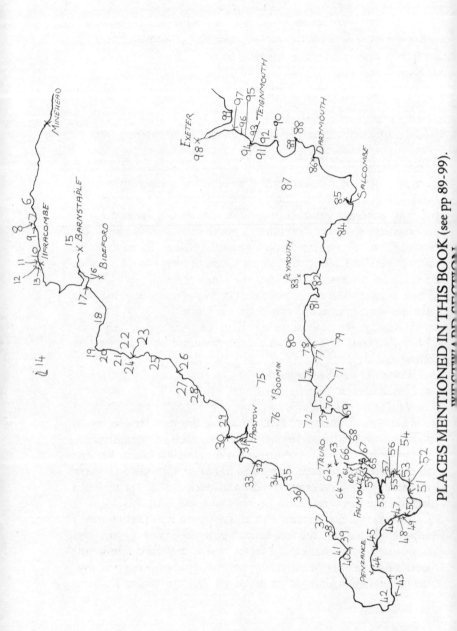

PLACES MENTIONED IN THIS BOOK (see pp 89-99).
WESTWARD SECTION

which proved fatal for the captain and crew of a smuggling lugger, which in order to avoid being seen by the riding officers on the cliff top, sailed too close inshore and was lost with all hands.

9   *Trentishoe.* In 1827, contraband landed at Heddon Mouth was hidden here on John Hoyle's farm. No less than 262 tubs were found under the stable floor. These were to be taken to Ilfracombe but the carters were attacked on the outskirts of the town and it was considered more expedient to take them to Barnstaple. Hoyle, a popular man in the locality, managed to avoid capture; and his wife was found not guilty of taking part in the venture.

10   *Watermouth.* More smugglers caves are to be seen here.

11   *Samson's Bay.* The name commemorates a famous local smuggler.

12   *Ilfracombe.* See pages 3, 33.

13   *Brandy Cove.* One of several place-names which proclaim their smuggling origin. It lies near Crewkhorne Cave, just west of Ilfracombe.

14   *Lundy.* See pages 3, 57 *et seq.*

15   *Barnstaple.* See pages 1, 58.

16   *Bideford.* See pages 3, 55.

17   *Appledore.* This little port was the scene of much smuggling activity. See page 34.

18   *Clovelly.* This village has long been associated with smuggling. The last vessel based there to be seized for smuggling was the thirty-seven-ton *Hope,* whose master, a man called Buckler, was arrested on 4th April, 1825. The caves off Hobby Drive and one to the north of the little harbour, which Clovelly children still call the Smugglers' Cave, were certainly used for hiding contraband. In fact, there is good reason to believe that the legend of the Clovelly Cannibals was deliberately put about to keep inquisitive people away from a cave full of contraband. (See *The Cannibals of Clovelly,* a little booklet published by the Bideford Community College in aid of the Clovelly Lifeboat.) The Red Lion was a famous smuggling inn. See pages 3, 24, 59.

19   *Hartland Point.* See pages 1, 57.

20   *Hartland Quay.* Associated with the smuggling activities of Edward Hockin. (See *Hartland Quay, The Story of a Vanished Port* an admirable piece of local history by Michael Nix and Mark R. Myers.) See also page 59.

21   *Sand Hole.* The site of Cruel Copinger's Cave.

22   *Henstridge Wood.* The site of Cruel Copinger's cache. See page 75.

23   *Steeple Point.* The site of another of Cruel Copinger's Caves.

24   *Morwenstowe.* The Bush is an old smuggling inn.

25   *Bude.* See page 34.

26   *St Genny's.* Wallett's Shute and Warristow were well-known local smuggling sites. See page 77.

27   *Crackington Haven.* This once remote creek was typical of those favoured by smugglers.

28   *Boscastle.* This charming little port was often used by smugglers, in spite of there being a coastguard station there, whose officers once captured 450 tubs, which had just been landed nearby. On that occasion a smuggling lugger recaptured the contraband and took the coastguard's boat as well.

29   *Port Isaac.* See page 77.

30   *Pentire.* See page 77.

31   *Padstow.* This port became famous for the ingenuity of its smugglers. One of the places a farmer used to hide contraband was beneath a gate post. Lisa Newcombe in *Smuggling in Cornwall and Devon* describes how contraband was hidden in the bedroom of a woman supposedly in labour. The doctor forbade the Customs officers to enter. See pages 3, 29, 33.

32   *Porth Cothan—Porth Maer.* This was the scene of many a successful run. The contraband was hidden in a cave 15 ft wide which led to a gallery 1,000 ft long, ending at Trevemeder Farm.

33   *Pepper Cove.* The name reminds us that brandy, tea, and tobacco were not the only things smuggled; while Wills' Rock commemorates the escape of a Revenue officer who was left to drown by smugglers but survived.

34 *Newquay.* Tea Caverns remind us of the vast quantities of smuggled tea which was drunk in the late eighteenth and early nineteenth centuries. See pages 11, 42.

35 *Crantock.* The Old Albion, four miles from Newquay, and Trebellion, two miles to the south, had strong smuggling connections, as the restaurant called The Smugglers Den suggests.

36 *Perranporth.* Here, according to Frank Pearce, a secret smuggling syndicate, which included both the Church of England parson and the Methodist minister, operated. They chartered their own ships and landed their contraband at Porth Cligga where it was hidden in caves.

37 *Portreath.* Hell's Mouth was the scene of a number of successful runs.

38 *Ralph's Cupboard.* This place got its name from the hide of a successful local smuggler.

39 *Hayle.* A lot of smuggling went on all round here, particularly at Godrevy. There is a secret passage, once used by smugglers, in the garden of Riviere House, now a Youth Hostel.

40 *Lelant.* Here the church was used for hiding contraband. Newcastle Cottage, once a famous kiddlywink on Trencrom Hill was a smugglers rendezvous, but is now in private hands.

41 *St Ives.* There were once three famous smuggling taverns in the town: The George & Dragon, The White Hart, and the Blue Bell Inn which was in St Andrew's Street, but is no longer a public house. See pages 2, 28, 33, 35.

42 *Sennen.* Joseph Pollard once landed 3,000 gallons of brandy here in one night, but he was captured. The only person to give evidence against him was Anne George, who had been landlady of The First and Last Inn, but her testimony was not accepted and Pollard was acquitted.

43 *Porth Gwarra to Mousehole.* At Paul Lane, between these two places, you will find the site of the murder of Martha Blewett, who, in 1792, when the duty was 6d, used to hawk contraband salt. Porth Gwarra was one of the places used by 'gentlemen smugglers', squires' sons who sailed over to Roscoff and brought back brandy

for a lark. So much smuggling went on at Mousehole that a force
of Revenue officers was stationed there. From 1832 to 1842 they
seized more than 300 tubs of spirit.

44   *Penzance.* The Dolphin was a favourite rendezvous for
smugglers. See pages 3, 33.

45   *Prussia Cove, Piskie's Cove, Bessie's Cove and King's Cove.* See
page 46 *et seq.*

46   *Porth Leven.* The Ship was a well-known smuggling inn.
There was once a tunnel leading from the caves on the west of the
harbour to Methleigh Manor, but it is now blocked. In the manor
house kitchen there was a contraband store under the floor and
other secret passages, now silted up, lead towards the coast.

47   *Gunwalloe.* Here a tunnel led from the belfry tower of the
church to a cave on the beach, now partially blocked, and cut off at
high tide. Two other caves used by smugglers are more accessible.
A secret passage is said to have led from The Halzephron Inn to
Fishing Cove.

48   *Fishing Cove and Dollar Cove.* The former was the home and
landing place of the famous smuggler Henry Cuttance. When he
was press-ganged he managed to escape from the man-of-war in
which he served by throwing his hat over one side of the ship,
shouting "Man overboard!" and jumping over the opposite
bulwarks. Close to the cliff top here is Helzephron House, where,
according to Frank Pearce, a tunnel leads to the cliff face, now
covered by a grill. Dollar Cove got its name from the ships
carrying 'pieces of eight' which were wrecked there.

49   *Mullion.* The home of two famous smugglers, Bobo George
and John Munday, who used a cavern called Torchlight Cave to
store their contraband. From it a tunnel is said to have led to a
cliff-top farm.

50   *Predannick, The Chair.* A favourite landing place of local
smugglers.

51   *Kennack Sands.* J. C. Corin of Coverack told me that
contraband used to be landed here.

52   *Black Head.* This was another site pinpointed as a landing place by J. C. Corin.

53   *Coverack.* The home of the famous Jack Corlyon. See pages 20, 36.

54   *Boat Road.* One of the alternative landing places for smugglers.

55   *Godrevey Cove.* Here there was a cave used by smugglers.

56   *Porthoustock.* Cyril Noall, in his admirable book *Smuggling in Cornwall,* writes that this little port was engaged in 'the trade'.

57   *Porthallow.* Thus small harbour is also mentioned by Cyril Noall. It lies a mile or so to the north.

58   *Gweek and Helford River.* The many creeks of the estuary provided a variety of alternative landing sites, which could not all possibly be covered by the Customs Service.

59   *Falmouth.* There are two caves and a neighbouring tunnel, all once used by smugglers, on the south side of the creek leading up to Penryn, at Wells Beach. The tunnel has now been blocked up. In the middle of the eighteenth century the mayor of Falmouth indulged in smuggling. See pages 11, 20, 30, 33.

60   *Penryn.* A tunnel is said to lead from St Gluvias Vicarage to the foreshore.

61   *Mylor.* This creek is typical of the places smugglers used for landing contraband. In the churchyard you will find the tomb of Thomas James who was shot by Customs officers.

62   *Tressillian Creek.* In 1701, at the very start of the period covered by this book, this place is described as 'a most convenient place for the smuggling of foreign goods'. It was then called Clement's Creek.

63   *Sunset Creek.* Cyril Noall lists Penpol Farm in this creek, opposite Malpas, as 'a good depot . . . where landed kegs were carried up a sunken road . . . and hidden in caves or in the woods'.

64   *Devoran.* See page 25.

65   *St Mawes.* The haunt of the famous seventeenth century smuggler, Robert Long. He was eventually hanged in chains on the road from St Mawes to Ruan Lanihorne.

66 *Tolverne.* To the north of St Mawes, where the ferry crosses the Fal, you will find Smuggler's Cottage, now a restaurant.

67 *Gerrans.* Here the smugglers were caught one night by an enterprising Customs officer who got his crew to row up Porth Creek, opposite St Mawes, to Froe, *and then carry their boat* about 300 yards overland to the coast.

68 *Portloe.* Smuggling activities here were sufficiently widespread for a Customs post to be established in 1824. Eighty-four tubs, sown in the cove, were retrieved by the Revenue men in 1843.

69 *Gorran Haven.* 130 kegs were seized by the Water Guard here in October 1825.

70 *Mevagissey.* One of the most famous smuggling centres. See pages 16, 42.

71 *St Austell Bay.* The waters here yielded a good crop for the Customs on several occasions. 250 tubs were retrieved between 1820 and 1832.

72 *Trewhiddle.* The Cornish home of Copinger. He may well have kept his boat at Mevagissey. See page 78 *et seq.*

73 *Pentewen.* The site of an attack on the Customs men by smugglers in 1815, which led to a reward of £200 being offered for their capture.

74 *Fowey.* The home of Richard Kingcup, the Revenue officer who turned smuggler and became landlord of The Crown and Anchor on the quay. See pages 3, 33.

75 *Jamaica Inn.* The smuggling inn at Bolventor on Bodmin Moor, made famous today by Daphne Du Maurier.

76 *Indian Queens.* Another inland smuggling site. See page 42.

77 *Polperro.* A place steeped in smuggling; and the home of Tom Potter, hanged for shooting a Revenue boatman, Humphrey Glinn, when trying to seize the smuggling lugger *Lottery*. He was betrayed by Roger Toms, who became the most hated man in Polperro. For the fullest authentic account of the *Lottery* affair, see *Smuggling in Cornwall* by Cyril Noall. In the village is a Smuggling Museum which should on no account be missed. See also pages 16, 35.

78 *Talland.* The churchyard here contained a memorial to Robert Mark of Polperro who was unfortunately shot at sea on 24th January, 1802, while engaged in smuggling.

79 *Looe and Looe Island.* This is where Black Joan and her brother Fyn operated. They received contraband on the island and transported it up Looe River. It was at The Jolly Sailor that the landlady sat on a keg of brandy to hide it from the search party. See also page 18.

80 *Duloe.* The church here was used to store so much contraband that the weight is said to have caused subsidence on one side.

81 *Whitsand Bay.* The scene of many smuggling episodes including much of the *Lottery* affair.

82 *Cawsand and Kingsand.* In 1804 the Customs at Plymouth estimated that 17,000 kegs had been landed at these twin ports. See pages 16, 25, 49.

83 *Plymouth.* This was not only the chief market for Cawsand contraband, it also provided a large number of smugglers from the ranks of sailors who had been discharged after the Napoleonic Wars. See also pages 17, 20, 26, 33.

84 *Burgh Island.* Tom Crocker was an early smuggler who not only used The Pilchard Inn, but also gave his name to a cave still known as Tom Crocker's Hole.

85 *Salcombe.* This became a favourite landing place for smugglers when Dartmouth suffered an epidemic of the plague. The church here was used as a hide.

86 *Dartmouth.* Even the Collector of Customs, Christopher Blackoller, took part in smuggling ventures. See also pages 3, 20, 33.

87 *Totnes.* The Bay Horse is said to have been a smuggling inn.

88 *Berry Head.* A cave here was used by the smuggler Bob Elliott of whom the same story is told as that of Resurrection Jackman. See page 67.

89 *Brixham.* The home of Resurrection Jackman.

90 *Torquay.* The cottage next to the Park Road Post Office in St Marychurch was used by smugglers.

91   *Rocombe.* A farm here had a hide up a large chimney.

92   *Maidencombe.* A farm with a secret doorway and a trap-door leading to a hide. Both these farms were inspected by Marjory Fielden and reported in the Transactions of the Devonshire Association.

93   *Shaldon.* Situated on the south bank of the Teign at its very mouth, this was also a favourite landing place for contraband.

94   *Combe Cellars.* Another landing place on a remote stretch of the Teign.

95   *Teignmouth.* Here you will find caves used by smugglers.

96   *Holcombe.* A Smuggler's Lane commemorates Free Trading.

97   *Dawlish Warren.* Although popular today this was another remote place in the eighteenth and nineteenth centuries, when contraband was hidden in the caves and The Mount Pleasant Inn was a smugglers' rendezvous.

98   *Exeter.* The Turk's Head is reputed to have been a smuggling inn. See pages 33, 42.

99   *Exmouth.* See page 44.

100 *Offwell.* See page 23.

101 *Wilmington.* The School House here also has a bottle set in the eastern gable end, signifying that the inhabitants were friendly to smugglers, as at nearby Batt's Close at Offwell.

102 *East Budleigh.* See page 24.

103 *Salcombe.* The church tower was used as a hide. See page 43.

104 *Branscombe.* The grave of John Hurley, Customs officer, is to be found here. The Three Horseshoes was a smuggling inn. See also pages 15, 24.

105 *Beer.* The home of Jack Rattenbury. See pages 5, 24, 38 *et seq.* Bovey House, now an hotel, see page 40.

106 *Sampford Peverell.* See page 23.

107 *Eggardon Hill.* See page 65.

108 *Worbarrow Bay.* The scene of many landings.

109 *Pondfield Caves.* Contraband was hidden here.

110 *Brandy Bay.* Another of those places which commemorate smuggling in their names.

111 *Dancing Ledge Cave.* One of the many smugglers' caves in the Isle of Purbeck.

112 *Tilly Whim Caves and Blackers Hole.* More examples of smugglers' hides.

113 *Langton Maltravers.* The church here was once used to store contraband.

114 *Ballard's Point.* More smugglers' caves will be seen here.

115 *Brownsea Island.* See page 62 *et seq.*

116 *Poole.* There is a small smuggling display in the museum. See pages 4, 63 *et seq.*

117 *Flag Pole Chine.* Favourite landing place for Isaac Gulliver's contraband. See page 66.

118 *Branksome Chine.* A deserted landing place before Bournemouth was built.

119 *Kinson.* See page 65.

120 *Horton Tower.* See page 65.

121 *West Moors.* Gulliver's Farm. See page 64.

122 *Smugglers' Lane.* As good a place as any to end this gazetteer. See page 23.

PLACES MENTIONED IN THIS BOOK (see pp 89-99).

BIBLIOGRAPHY

RESEARCH leads one to delve in strange fields. Tombstones and cigarette cards have provided material for this book as well as maps, newspaper files, pamphlets, and other volumes. The three dozen books listed below have all been entertaining and interesting, and so are worth perusing. Some are serious works and merit careful study.

Acton, H. and Holland, H. H., *The King's Customs*, London, 1908, 1967

Browning, H. J., *They Didn't Declare It*, 1967

Carson, E., *The Ancient and Rightful Customs*, London, 1972

Carter, Captain Harry, *The Autobiography of a Cornish Smuggler*, (1894), Truro, 1971

Chacksfield, K. M., *Smuggling Days*, Christchurch, 1968

Coxhead, J. R. W., *Smuggling Days in Devon*, Exmouth, 1956

Dowling, R. F. W., *Smuggling on Wight Island*, Ventnor, 1978

Farjeon, J. Jefferson, *The Complete Smuggler*, London, 1959

Farquharson-Coe, A., *Hants and Dorset Smugglers*. nd

Foster, D. Arnold, *At War with the Smugglers*, London, 1936

Graham, Frank, *Cornish Smugglers Tales*, Newcastle, 1967

„   „   *Smuggling in Devon*, Newcastle, 1965

„   „   *Famous Smuggling Inns*, Newcastle, 1966

„   „   *More Smuggling Inns*, Newcastle, 1969

Hardy, Clive R., *The Smuggler's Guide to Purbeck*. Bristol, nd

Harper, Charles G., *Haunted Houses*, London, 1907

Keeble-Chatterton, E., *King's Cutters and Smugglers*, 1908

Newcombe, Lisa, *Smuggling in Cornwall and Devon*, Norwich, 1975

Nicholls, F., *Honest Thieves*, London, 1973

Nix, Michael, and Myers, M. R., *Hartland Quay*, Hartland, 1982

Noall, Cyril, *Smuggling in Cornwall*, Truro, 1971

Oakley, E. Russell, *The Smugglers of Christchurch, Bourne Heath and the New Forest*, London, 1943

Parnall, Roger, *Wreckers and Wrestlers*, 1973

Phillipson, D., *Smuggling, A History 1700-1970*, Newton Abbot, 1973

Rattenbury, John, *Memoirs of a Smuggler*, Sidmouth, 1937

Shore, Lieut the Hon. Henry, *Smuggling Days and Smuggling Ways*

Shore, Cmdr the Hon. Henry, *Smugglers of Fowey*, (1907) Newcastle, 1966

Smith, Graham, *Something to Declare*, London, 1980

Squires, Granville, *Secret Hiding Places*

Sutton, Harry T., *Honest Rogues*, London, 1978

Tanguy, Jean-Yves, *Le Port et Havre de Roscoff*, La Baule, 1975

Teignmouth, Lord, and Harper, Charles, *The Smugglers*, London, 1923

Thomas, Stanley, *The Nightingale Scandal*, Bideford, 1959

Verrill, A. Hyatt, *Smugglers and Smuggling*, New York, 1924

Vivian, John, *Tales of the Cornish Smuggler*, Truro, nd

Warneford, R., *Tales of the Coastguard*, 1856

Williams, Neville, *Contraband Cargoes*, London, 1959

The files of the *Exeter Flying Post*, the *Royal Cornwall Gazette*, and the *Sherborne Mercury* also provided valuable material.